LANDLESS PEOPLE:
BUILDING A SOCIAL MOVEMENT

MARTA HARNECKER

LANDLESS PEOPLE:
BUILDING A SOCIAL MOVEMENT

EDITORA
EXPRESSÃO POPULAR

Graphic Design:
Zap Design

Cover Art:
Vince Antonysen

Photos:
Carlos Carvalho, Douglas Mansur and Maria Luisa Mendonça

Translation:
Maria Carla Bassegio

Printed and Finished:
Cromosete

ISBN: 85-87394-38-X

First edition, january 2003

EDITORA EXPRESSÃO POPULAR
Rua Bernardo da Veiga, 14
CEP 01252-020 - São Paulo - SP
e-mail: editora@expressaopopular.com.br
www.expressaopopular.com.br

INDEX

PREFACE TO A DIFFERENT KIND OF BOOK BY MARTA HARNECKER ON THE MOVEMENT OF LANDLESS PEASANTS

Miguel Urbano Rodriguez [1]

*L*andless People – Building a Social Movement [2] is a striking book.

The author draws the reader on a walk across an unknown world, an emotional trip full of permanent surprises.

The subject of the Movement of Landless Workers (MST) has become practically a legend. A lot is said about it, but not much is known.

---

[1] Portuguese writer and journalist. He has been a member of the Parliamentary Assemblies of the Council of Europe and the Union of Western Europe and, previously, he was the main editorialist of the Brazilian newspaper *O Estado de São Paulo*.

[2] This book by Marta Harnecker will soon be published by the Siglo XXI España Publishing House.

Important works have been published in Brazil on the MST, among them the interview-book Brava Gente (Brave People) in which the most outstanding leader of the Movement, João Pedro Stedile, evoques its history within the context of the struggles of Brazilian society.

Marta Harnecker's book now fills the need for more extensive qualified foreign bibliography on the MST. Her study comes in response to an intense curiosity about an organization still veiled in mystery for millions of people.

With the same methodology and the rigor we are used to expect in her information, this Chilean sociologist recurs to a sober yet communicative style to throw light on the stage where this struggle is being waged by a movement that followed nonviolent paths to progressively acquire its own personal dynamics. Today it appears more and more like an instrument for revolutionary changes in Brazilian society. The actors of this atypical ongoing revolution receive the author's special attention.

All this, in a country/continent where some *fazendas* cover more than one million hectares of land – the surface of the largest being equal to Belgium's: 30 000 square kilometers. I mention this fact only to help the reader realize that the word *latifundium* is an understatement and prevents the full understanding of a reality framed in tragedy: the secular hunger for land of those peasants who do not possess it.

According to Marta, "the only way out for the landless peasants is to look for different actions that would allow them to procure land wherever they lived – especially if we take into account the fact that in all regions of the country there was more than enough uncultivated land. [...] Occupation of the land then becomes the main instrument of pressure and the first school for the political awareness and the socialization of thousands of peasants."

Throughout the 17 years since its foundation, the MST has been able to settle some 350 000 peasant families and 100 000 more are distributed in 500 camps, "waiting for their time to come."

The author of *Elementary Concepts of Historical Materialism*[3] would have been unable to write this book if she had not reached a deep understanding of the men and women who made this saga of the MST possible.

The conquest of the land would have amounted to nothing if the peasants had not fought all these years, creating the conditions to work it. The fact is that they lacked everything: machinery, seeds, cattle, credit, technical know-how, trade outlets.

More obstacles came to worsen this reality. The large landowners – perhaps the most reactionary agrarian oligarchy in Latin America – felt this menace and unleashed a real war against the MST, using criminal methods, often with the complicity of governmental leaders. Marta describes how these landless workers, with the same discipline of a weaponless army, opposed their resistance to all sorts of things: persecutions, expulsions from occupied lands, aggressiveness of both policemen and gunmen, imprisonment and torture, assaults and fires in trade-union offices, collective murders, even false trials based on invented evidence.

In spite of this atmosphere of hate and terror, the MST grew and in less than two decades, became "the main national reference for the struggle against neoliberalism, promoting actions of several sectors excluded by the system: the landless, the homeless, and those with no work."

If Marta Harnecker had adopted the stand of an academic researcher, she would have been unable to write a book like this, in which the reader enters action like in a film, feeling both the dimension and the force of the challenge of the landless workers, the terrible sufferings of the pioneers of the Movement and the

---

[3] Published by Siglo XXI, Mexique, Spain, 62 editions, with more than one million copies sold in Spanish-speaking countries, and translated into French, English, Portuguese and Greek.

tenacity of the generation that adopted the project, thus guaranteeing its continuity. She chose another path. She understood that the study of the documents on the Movement, the works in files and libraries would never be able to substitute the direct and intimate contact with the actors of this epic poem.

The writer went directly into the battlefield. She visited camps, sank in the mud and dust of the settlements and *agrovilas,* shared the lives of peasant leaders in Rio Grande do Sul, Santa Catarina, Paraná, São Paulo, Bahia, Mato Grosso and Pernambuco. Once she had won their trust, she listened to the stories they all tell, authentic chapters of the larger, dramatic and beautiful history of the landless peasants of Brazil.

This experience, this vision and the interpretation that came out of the long nights spent in the company of peoples with very different cultures and habits, according to the states they came from, helped Marta overcome that wall of misunderstanding that makes a true mystery of what they call *mística.*

And in the end, what is this *mística* all about?

Some see in it a kind of religious sentiment with pantheistic shades. Marta explains it as the expression of the moral force and faith in the victory of the landless workers, the belief of these peasants that man is a solidary being. It is mainly this belief that allows them to feel – even if their scientific-ideological basis is not yet solid – that socialism is the only alternative to the capitalist neoliberal social order that oppresses them. The MST cultivates spiritual attitudes in all its collective activities. "Song, theater, poetry, dance, images – all have important roles together with the MST symbols: their flag, their anthem."

We have before us an existentialist attitude that explains, for example, the Ten Ethical Commandments, a code that condenses the commitment of the MST with both the land and life.

Irma Brunetto, one of their leaders, first explains how this force emanating from their solidary feelings led them to seemingly unattainable social and economic victories, such as the increase in some of the MST settlements of the yield per hectare in comparison to that of modern *fazendas*, in products requiring complex technologies, and then, in an enlightening confession, she states: "The MST became a sort of State. We do what the State should do, and a lot more."

I don't believe Irma is exaggerating. Her words reflect the Movement's wish to transform things in a revolutionary way.

One of Marta Harnecker's great merits was her capacity to transmit a very difficult idea: the stirring stage of the enormous battle in which the MST peasants are writing history, following this long road whose main victories are the result of imagination, firm positions, study and discipline – attitudes that allowed them to overcome their errors and become a source of teachings and creativity.

There are many weak points in the MST: there is always a gap between reality and dreams. The testimonies gathered by Marta do not hide these difficulties – on the contrary, they are explained crudely. And yet, hope is strengthened as a result of the will of the Movement to face them.

In order to provide strong evidence for many aspects of the MST's daily fight that seem to come out of a novel based on magical realism – such as the symbiosis between school and camp or settlement, which opens the doors to an ongoing educational revolution – in some chapters Marta abandoned her usual literary technique, though not her style. To express the internal world of the actors of what she interpreted to be a modern epic, this social scientist felt the need to alter the way in which she communicates as a writer. She changed both her form and her language. In many of these pages the word became an instrument and a channel for the emotions and feelings that the dry narrative of an essay would have been unable to transmit.

In this beautiful book, the reader is stirred by the actors of the marvelous yet difficult human adventure the MST is living on the road leading to tomorrow. Road, life and dreams melt harmoniously into an odyssey. Words become human, and sometimes what we have before us is the rhythm, the beauty and the mystery of a poem written in prose.

Marta Harnecker has written a very important book on a social movement that will leave a deep impression on the history of man's millenary struggle for the land.

INTRODUCTION

The Movement of Landless Rural Workers of Brazil (MST) is without any doubt one of the most important social movements in Latin America.

It was developed under the influence of progressive sectors of different Christian currents – the most outstanding being the Catholic Church's Pastoral of the Land – a few years after the Sandinista victory in Nicaragua and its multiplying effects on the continent's revolutionary movement. After long years of military dictatorship, Brazil was enjoying new democratic breezes. Manifestations of popular dissatisfaction were on the upsurge, in particular important trade-union struggles on the outskirts of São Paulo; they were the original starting point for the Workers' Party and later, the Single Workers' Trade Union.

This situation was unleashed, among other things, by the incipient crisis in the economic model implemented by the military. As a result of this crisis, the peasants – driven from their lands by droughts and poverty in both the North and West-Central regions, as well as by capitalist modernization of the countryside in the Central and Southern part of the country – had increasingly fewer possibilities of finding work in the cities. On the other hand and for different reasons, emigration to the regions of agricultural colonization (1) had not worked out as a solution. It became more and more evident that the only way out for the landless peasants was to look for different actions that would allow them to procure land wherever they lived – especially taking into account that there was more than enough uncultivated land in all regions of the country.

The first seizures of land are motivated by this situation, and they are so successful that they increase during the following years. A growing number of peasant families begin to understand that they will conquer the land only through struggle. Occupation of the land then becomes the main instrument of pressure and the first school for the political awareness and the socialization of thousands of peasants. The MST has thus been able to accumulate in this field a high degree of practical knowledge: 17 years after its foundation, it has been able to settle some 350 000 peasant families through this method and yet another 100 000 are distributed in about 500 camps all over Brazil, waiting for their time to come.

But the Movement is aware that it is not enough to conquer the land and settle the peasant families; it must also create conditions for them to work it and obtain the necessary benefits for their survival. Without machinery, seeds, credits, technical know-how to allow them to use the modern techniques of the technological revolution; with no outlets for their products, instead of becoming a space for freedom, the land would become a nightmare and they would end up selling it at very low prices, or simply abandoning it. That is why the MST insists on the fact that the struggle does not end with the conquest of the land – they must keep fighting in an organized way to meet the other objectives.

---

[1] Places on the agricultural frontier where the government promotes peasant presence.

To be successful in this new stage of the struggle, it is very important for the peasants to continue their organization and articulation within the Movement. Experience has shown that the best way to organize at the base is in groups of 20 to 30 families. The MST has suggested that once the land is conquered, the settlements should continue with this kind of organization, and that these groups of families should gather in small rural communities or *agrovilas* (rural villages), where the houses would be close to each other and there would be areas for collective services, such as the school, recreational centers, a small park, the kindergarten etc. This suggestion, however, has not always become a reality. In most cases, Incra (2) proposed that the land be distributed on an individual basis. The families ended up far from each other and this hindered their mutual relations. That is why the Movement is now studying other solutions that will allow the peasants to live on their own piece of land, while leading a collective life with a group of families.

The MST also has another challenge: how to combine the existence of these groups of families – that allow for a better organization and participation – with the need to make a local impact, aimed at changing – at least at that level – the rules of the game prevailig in the countryside. The idea has come up, as part of the solution to this contradiction, to create what some people have defined as *pólos de assentamentos* (settlement concentrations). This concentration of numerous settlements in one territory would allow, among other things, for the implementation of an alternative people's market in the region, which would trade the products of their agricultural cooperatives.

Though they are a minority and are subject to multiple limitations – because they are inserted in a system governed by the rule of profits – the more developed settlements, together with their *agrovilas* and

---

[2] National Institute for Colonization and Agrarian Reform.

agro-industries, represent true showcases for the just and solidary society that the Movement places at the horizon of their struggles.

It has not been easy to plan and organize production to guarantee the survival of the families in the settlements and increase their incomes wherever possible: frequently, the lands allotted are low quality, or eroded because the large landowners have not worked them correctly. On top of all this, these areas usually have very poor and deficient infrastructures.

To overcome these difficulties, the MST has implemented different ways of cooperation, the most developed being agricultural and cattle-breeding cooperatives. Though the existence of a state system for agricultural credits benefited those already organized under this method and stimulated this option, the difficulties have been larger than expected. Model cooperatives have been built in some places, but a majority of them have had serious problems as a result of their lack of experience, errors, and the limitations imposed by the existing economic system. Easy credits tied to a specific technological pattern paved the way for the kind of mechanization that did not correspond to the peasants' needs.

Instead of diversifying production, they chose to work with just one product, thus endangering them seriously because of market variations. Existing legislation and the laws of the market became very complicated obstacles.

As was to be expected, the combative attitude of this movement has unleashed a fierce resistance from the large Brazilian landowners – one of the most reactionary social classes in the world. They have used all possible means to stop the Movement: from persecutions and attemps on the lives of workers and their leaders, to the use of gunmen and state police corps to throw the peasants off the land, murdering whole families peacefully devoted to working the land, throwing them into prison and torturing them; in the larger *fazendas,* kidnappings and slavery; in trade-union offices, force and fire; unfounded accusations of murder against people who had not even been present at the scene of the crime; physical extermination of workers, leaders and agents of the Christian pastorals devoted to the struggle for the land.

In spite of all these attempts to ignore it, isolate it, repress it, coopt it, drown it economically, destroy its image in the mass media and confuse its social base by means of a systematic campaign of misinformation, the MST has continued to grow and consolidate itself. It is now the main national reference point for the struggle against neoliberalism, promoting actions of several sectors excluded by the system: the landless, the homeless, and those with no work.

Notwithstanding attacks from the right because of its radical position, the Movement has achieved increasing respect from growing sectors of society. They now recognize in it the political coherence and interest for ideological aspects frequently absent from leftist political parties. We must recognize, however, that the occupation of public buildings in the cities, to make their struggle more visible and exert pressure for land, credits and other demands, is not well seen by middle-class sectors, influenced by images of disorder published by the mass media to undermine their prestige.

The Movement is open to all good ideas, no matter where they come from, and it jealously defends its autonomy in relation to other institutions. Strongly influenced by progressive religious currents and clearly committed to the struggles of rural workers, it does not submit to any kind of outside leadership. It stresses the political commitment of its members, but does not want to be the link with parties from the left, even though a majority of its members vote for the Workers' Party and many of them are active militants in it.

There are two significant elements that contribute to this autonomy: the financial policy of the Movement and the way it educates its cadres. As far as the financial policy is concerned, contrary to many leftist movements and parties that depend mainly on their participation in other institutions and outside assistance, the MST finances its own needs. The peasants who have already received land

and credit to work it support the Movement with a percentage of their resources and a quota of their production. On the other hand, different forms of cooperation implemented by many settlements in their production free some of the cadres from other responsibilities to work only on militant tasks for the Movement. As far as the second aspect is concerned, the MST considers that a movement will be autonomous only if it is able to form its own cadres – hence its insistence on the creation of special schools at different levels.

Within the Movement discipline is exceptionally strong, not as a result of a militarist and authoritarian policy but rather of correct methods of leadership. Narrow majorities are avoided; rather than impose criteria, persuasion is preferred. And they postpone the adoption of all decisions if the movement as a whole is not ripe enough for them.

Aware that the weak link in many movements and parties is their dependence on a reduced number of leaders, the MST tries to develop a collective leadership strongly connected to the base. The kind of leader who uses the bus whenever possible, instead of traveling by plane throughout this huge country; who limits and rotates trips to foreign countries so that all its members will have equal opportunities, thus avoiding the creation of career diplomats. Another important aspect is that the leaders, from any instance whatsoever, undergo a critical evaluation every two years, and their mandate is renewed if the whole group considers that their contribution is still valuable for the Movement.

Aware of the fact that Brazil is a country of huge contrasts, yet understanding that a national network of peasant struggles in the various regions is a key factor against those who oppose a radical agrarian reform, the Movement tries to link the different struggles in a single column, while respecting the differences not only in each individual region but also among its own members, thus avoiding the imposition of organizational and action formulas that do not take these differences into account.

Another noteworthy aspect is the fact that in spite of its being a peasant movement with a strong machista gene, it has achieved a high participation of women in its activities. A good example of this participation is the fact that of the 23 members in the highest echelon, nine are women, elected because of their merits and not on a quota system.

Women have slowly come into leading roles in different spheres, without sacrificing their families. In camps and settlements, courses and meetings, conditions have been created so that the mothers can participate while their children are attended to. No solution has yet been found, however, for married women with children who occupy leading roles. In fact, of the nine women belonging to the National Leadership, only two are married, with no children; another group is made up of women separated from their companions; and another are unmarried mothers.

This social movement has a huge moral force and faith in victory; all those who approach it are touched by its happiness and confidence in the future. In my opinion, this is due to their conviction that socialism is the alternative to present-day capitalist neoliberal order, stressing its utopic aspects more than the real difficulties suffered by the countries that implemented it. But it is also due to their firm decision to fight against the injustices of the capitalist system, and their belief that man is imbued with solidarity. The spiritual aspect of the people is cultivated by the Movement in all its collective activities. That is what they call mystique. Song, theater, poetry, dance, images – all of them have important roles to play together with the MST symbols: their flag, their anthem. All are the expression of a collective feeling that unites, identifies and strengthens their spirit of resistance and struggle.

There is still a long road ahead, because the cultural transformation of its social base – made up of rural workers brought up on individualistic patterns and with a very low cultural level – cannot come about overnight, yet I believe that what has already been achieved in these 17 years of struggle is a source of inspiration and learning for those popular movements in different parts of the world that are just setting out on this road with increasing strength.

It is true that the peasants organized within the MST have achieved their goals only partially; yet one of their major victories has been the possibility of working for their own good, not being forced to work for others; guaranteeing education for their children, and – perhaps the most important aspect of all – acquiring dignity: today they consider themselves equal citizens with the rest of the world, not pariahs of society.

The purpose of this book is to describe the essential aspects of this experience, underlining those elements that, in my opinion, can be more useful to all those who want to organize themselves and fight for a society with more justice and solidarity. I have divided the book into five chapters: History, Occupations and Camps, Settlements, Education, and Internal Organization. The initial and detailed index reflects the different aspects of the contents.

At the beginning, I had decided not to use interviews, since I was aware that the organization had published many documents, the majority of which were very instructive. I believed it would be quicker to gather and organize what was already written and complete the existing information with a few interviews. That is really how I started working, but as soon as I circulated a preliminary version of what I believed to be an almost complete book – as I usually do with everything I write – my critical readers sent me two opinions that worried me: the first was related to the fact that not everything was as great as I described it; the second one believed that I generalized what occurred in one region of Brazil to the rest of the country, the truth being that each region had a very different reality.

In order to overcome these weak points, I decided to do more research into the processes behind the solutions described in books.

I then decided to carry out several interviews that would tell me how each process came about, what difficulties were encountered on the way, how they overcame them, which ideas were left behind. Some of the people interviewed told me about their own experiences, thus making this information easy and interesting for the reader. Others talked about the difficulties and teachings they confronted while following this path. Thanks to these opinions I learned a lot about the agrarian problems and the challenges facing these people, in their efforts to create a cooperative world in the present-day context. But above all, I became increasingly convinced of the importance of the method we use in the Research Center Latin-American People's Memory (MEPLA), of which I am the director in Cuba. If we want to learn something about the left and social movements, we cannot refer only to written documents. They tend to petrify ideas, as though they had no history, and to confuse with reality what is nothing but a project. I am convinced that we must try to reconstruct the processes, as the only way to get a better understanding of events. We must know about their projects, what part of them has materialized, and why the other part has not; describe the distortions produced while implementing these projects and the new ideas that came up along the way. I believe that is the only way we can then contribute to people's education – in other words, that other people may learn from this experience and thus avoid the same errors and distortions. To stress even more the idea that we are talking about processes that acquire their own personality according to the different realities in which they develop, I decided to incorporate two testimonies on what we might define the "life history" of two settlements, from the day they first camped until now. It will be up to the reader to say if we achieved our aim.

I would like to explain that I am aware of the fact that the book puts more emphasis on the experiences of South Brazil. That does not mean I prefer that region, but rather it is due to an objective reality: that is where the MST has achieved its greater development, and somehow these experiences have been a reference point for other regions of the country.

Natalia Alvarez, a young Argentinian-Paraguayan researcher, was a close collaborator for this book; and Maria Almeida, Brazilian researcher, transcribed the interviews and was my main support in Brazil. I would also like to thank the members of the MST for their opinions and suggestions, from the camps up to the national level, and all of the MEPLA work team for their cooperation, in particular Carlos García Pleyán and Berta Menéndez, who has been in charge of the final edition of this book.

Marta Harnecker
Havana, January 4, 2002

CHAPTER ONE

HISTORY OF THE MST

I – IMMEDIATE BACKGROUND

The Movement of Landless Rural Workers (MST) in Brazil inherited a prolonged struggle for land that goes back to the arrival of the Portuguese to the country. We will refer here only to the more immediate background: the first peasant movements organized in the 1950s and the effect the 1964 military coup had on them.

Between 1950 and 1964 three important peasant organizations struggling for land and agrarian reform came up: the *Ligas Camponesas* (Peasant Leagues), the Ultabs (1) and the Master. (2)

Peasant Leagues

The Peasant Leagues started forming around 1945, when Vargas' dictatorship was coming to an end. (3) They included peasants who owned their land, sharecroppers (4), occupants, and *meeiros* (5) who resisted being expelled from their lands to work on a salary system. They were created in practically all states and at one given point in time they organized thousands of peasants. They were supported by the Communist Party of Brazil (PCB), on which they depended.

In 1947, when the Dutra government declared the PCB illegal, they were brutally repressed. Seven years later, they reappeared in Pernambuco, with the support of Francisco Julião, lawyer and deputy of the Brazilian Socialist Party, who became their leader. From that date on, new Leagues were formed in that and other states of Northeast Brazil, as well as in other regions. In 1962 they existed in 13 states and had already organized several meetings and congresses. (6)

Their ideological and political influence came from different leftist parties and groups, and they became well-known because they took over several sugar mills; because they exerted influence on the election of Miguel Arraes as progressive governor in Pernambuco; and because of the continuous pressure of the masses on Goulart's government to implement a law of agrarian reform.

In time, their struggle of resistance against the large landowners who wanted to expel them from their lands became increasingly strong. Several peasants died in that conflict. In 1962 João Pedro Texeira, founder of the Sape League – the biggest in the country – was murdered.

The Peasant Leagues were undoubtedly the most massive and radical movement of the struggle for agrarian reform at that time. (7) They resisted expulsion and went on to occupy the lands, while the Catholic Church and the PCB still defended an agrarian reform divided in different stages, which would include compensation and property titles.

Part of the Leagues tried to organize guerrilla groups; many workers were made prisoner and the army dispersed the groups. They finally disappeared with the 1964 military coup.

Ultabs

In 1954, while the Peasant Leagues were reappearing in

Pernambuco, the PCB created the Union of Farmers and Agricultural Workers (Ultab), a sort of association of rural workers organized at the municipal, state and national levels, to coordinate peasant associations. With this initiative, the PCB sought to create conditions for a political alliance between workers and peasants. This organization covered all states except for Pernambuco and Rio Grande do Sul, where other peasant bodies were already strong. They penetrated mainly the states of São Paulo, Paraná and Rio de Janeiro.

At the same time, in an attempt to avoid the influence of socialist ideas over the peasant world and hoisting agrarian reform as their banner, the conservative sector of the Catholic Church organized in Rio Grande do Norte a Rural Assistance Service, founding dozens of unions and organizing up to 40 000 peasants.

Meanwhile, the progressive sector of the Catholic Church founded the Movement for Education at the Base, with the participation of Paulo Freire, an educator who worked in literacy campaigns and political education for the peasants.

Master

Finally, but on a smaller scale, at the end of the 1950s, in the state of Rio Grande do Sul the Movement of Landless Farmers (Master) appeared, resisting the eviction of 300 families who had occupied land in Encruzilhada do Sul. Later it grew all over the state with the support of governor Leonel Brizola, who had been able to take over several *fazendas*.

What made the Master different from the Leagues was that the workers in its ranks did not fight to stay on the land but to conquer a piece of land. From 1962 on they started to organize camps close to the latifundia's fences. The support of the government lasted until 1962. With the defeat of the Brazilian Labor Party (PTB) in that year's elections, the movement became increasingly weak and disappeared with the military coup. (8)

Attempts at unionizing

In 1961 the Ultabs had held their First National Congress of Farmers and Agricultural Workers in Belo Horizonte. Fourteen hundred workers participated, including 215 delegates from the Peasant Leagues and 50 from the Master. The more radical proposals of the Peasant Leagues won at that meeting, over those of the PCB. Their proposals set forth the need to promote unionizing, create labor legislation, and implement a campaign for salaries and the right to social security. This congress gave a great impetus to the struggles for land.

On account of this development of peasant organizations they did not control, the government and some institutions working with the peasants thought of creating unions to regulate rural unionizing as a way to channel and, in some cases, subordinate and weaken the movement. Local and state meetings were arranged to conform a future federation of rural workers. The PCB and the Catholic Church fought over this space, and after several attempts by both sides to take over the process, they finally reached an agreement in December 1963 to create the National Confederation of Agricultural Workers (Contag).

The Peasant Leagues, severely repressed at the time, did not participate in this process of unionizing.

II – Dictatorship and setback for the peasant movement (1964-1978)

In March 1964 the military coup took place. The dictatorship "violently repressed all the peasant movements alleging they were a communist menace. The main leaders were imprisoned, many had to go into exile, and hundreds of other leaders were murdered. Terror was installed in Brazil. Anyone speaking about agrarian reform was a candidate for several months in prison. [...] Repression was so harsh that the three [peasant] movements [already mentioned] were destroyed. Some unions of rural workers put up a very weak resistance but they completely changed their activities and came to assume the characteristics of a social assistance organization." (9)

This social aspect of the unions was strengthened when general Médici created Funrural in 1971 – a social security fund for the countryside – and transferred its bureaucratic activities to the unions. Today many of them are still considered delegations of Funrural. (10)

The 1960s ended with the pacification of the countryside. "Peace from the graveyard. Thousands of rural workers from the Northeast and the South, who had dreamed of agrarian reform and had taken steps to organize themselves into social movements to achieve it, saw their dreams shattered under the military boot." (11)

"At the beginning of the dictatorship, the military had created the Statute of the Land (12), with the idea of giving an isolated solution to the conflicts related to the land, thus demobilizing the peasants. Their aim was to prevent the agrarian question from becoming a national problem."(13)

III – GENERAL CONTEXT IN WHICH THE MST WAS BORN

Let us now examine the general context behind the birth of the MST.

Economic context

Capitalist modernization in the countryside took place during the 1970s, bringing with it a thorough and quick mechanization of agricultural exploitation, particularly in the South, directing it toward agricultural exports already controlled by powerful transnational corporations.

This stage is also known as "conservative" or "painful modernization," because it provoked a social and economic disaster for families of rural origin.

The introduction of soybean plantations accelerated

mechanization in the countryside. As a result of the most advanced technologies applied to this crop, masses of peasants were expelled from their lands. Machinery took over the work of sharecroppers and tenant farmers in coffee and cotton plantations in the South and Southeast, thus creating masses of landless peasants.

Particularly between 1975 and 1980, these farmers had to look for individual solutions, migrating to large cities or areas of agricultural colonization.

In the first case, they were attracted by the accelerated process of industrialization – this was the period known as the "Brazilian miracle" – but very soon the dream faded away. The first signs of industrial crisis appeared at the end of the 70s, and together with it, unemployment grew in the cities, where there was no longer any work for the peasants emigrating there. (14)

In the second case, those who migrated toward areas of agricultural colonization – particularly in the states of Rondonia, Pará and Mato Grosso – were attracted by official propaganda that promised an abundance of land. But problems came up immediately: there were no roads, no means of production, and no welfare. Abandoned to their fate, the emigrants were unable to preserve their peasant status. These territories lacked conditions for a family agricultural production of grains and other staple foods. The government, on the other hand, was looking for a labor force to promote the exploitation of metals, precious stones and wood, with the added strategic idea of settling huge numbers of people on Brazil's international frontiers.

Very soon, these already precarious work conditions were intensified by the menace of expulsion from the land by the big transnational corporations that began to settle in those regions. Property-owners and businessmen from the South, "stimulated by the government's fiscal incentives (the possibility of using on *fazendas* of the region money corresponding to income tax) started buying property titles of land in the Amazonic region." But since "much of the land coveted by the corporations was already occupied by workers, the majority of whom had no property titles," a new kind of struggle for the land appeared: the resistance of the occupants, or *posseiros*, against the action of the property-owners and the corporations who were trying to expel them. Thus conflicts and aggressions increased, the majority of them ending in death and destruction by fire of their plantations and households. (15)

The dreams of hundreds of thousands of peasants who had emigrated to those distant places in their search for a piece of land were now shattered.

From a socio-economic point of view, this is how they shut down the two doorways used by those peasants who had been expelled from the land as a result of agricultural mechanization: either migrate to the cities, or move to areas with agricultural frontiers. (16)

This situation generated the need to find a third solution: the attempt at resisting in the countryside and the search for methods of struggle that would allow the peasants to obtain land where they lived. (17)

Those peasants who chose this last option became the social base for the MST. (18)

Social and political context

Process of democratization of the country

On the other hand, since the so-called "Brazilian miracle" was no longer a miracle and the economy of the country was losing speed, the military regime became increasingly weaker and the country started out on a process of democratization. People began to show their discontent, concentrating first on human rights, but very soon they had other demands and became stronger as a result of important union struggles outside São Paulo, the origin of the Workers' Party (PT).

Combative rural unionism (19)

In this context, the peasants began to lose their fear; there was rural union opposition and some nuclei of combative unionism. (20) They criticized the assistive nature of the official unions, which had been reinforced with the creation of the social security fund already mentioned, destined for the countryside, and opposed the agricultural policies of the government. Finally these groups ended up joining the Single Workers' Trade Union (CUT).

For decades, the federal government had tried to make the union movement one of its appendages, granting it a series of privileges and attempting to orient its path toward an assistive and service unionism. Rural unions had dentists, doctors, sold selected seeds and veterinarian products.

Official unionism helped multiply the green revolution, which consisted in the use of selected seeds, chemical fertilizers, medicines for animals and other products, all made by transnational corporations.

"Combative rural unionism" preferred to activate the union structure from within. It introduced the aspect of social struggle, and from the very beginning this aspect put it on friendly terms with the incipient MST. Many of its leaders participated in its first events. They say that 80% of those present at the Movement's First National Meeting were union leaders. (21)

Ideological context: influence of the church pastorals

From the mid 70s on, the ideological aspect was being fertilized by the work that, under the inspiration of Theology for Liberation, the Catholic Church's Pastoral Commission for the Land (CPT) (22) had carried out. Priests and laymen together traveled around the countryside proclaiming the need for the peasants to organize and struggle, and solve their problems not in heaven, but here on earth.

On the other side, thanks to the CPT's ecumenism (23), they

were able to join their efforts with other churches, thus contributing to the development of a single movement.

In a word: the sudden increase in the concentration of the property of the land and the growing number of landless rural workers; the reduction of alternatives that might improve this situation, which unleashed both lack of security and misery among a population already used to living within a certain level of stability; the influence of the progressive pastorals of different churches and the process of democratization going on in the country – all made up the framework within which, slowly yet decisively, spontaneous initiatives for the occupation of the land appeared. This is how they laid the social base for consolidation of the MST.

IV – STRUGGLES THAT PAVED THE WAY FOR ITS BIRTH (1978-1984)

We could say that there is a period for the creation of the Landless Movement that goes from 1978, when struggles for the land resumed in the South – where repression had been less intense – up to 1984, when the MST was founded. The first sparks came on fire in Rio Grande do Sul.

Struggles in the south

Macali and Brilhante
In May 1978, the indigenous community of Kaigang, of the Indigenous Reserve at Nonoai, began action to recover their territories, expelling 1200 small peasant families who had settled on their lands. Each expelled family looked for its own solution. Some went to relatives' homes in another municipality; 50 migrated to Porto Alegre, looking for employment, and ended up living outside the city. Three large groups camped at the roadside: one in the town of Cruzeiro, in the Planalto Municipality; another at the

border of the Reserve, in the Nonoai Municipality; and the third, in the town of Três Palmeiras, a district in Ronda Alta. These three groups were organized in such a way that they started to look for support. Some militants from the left, who made up a group backing agrarian reform in Porto Alegre, started visiting them and carrying out political work with them.

The families who had camped in Três Palmeiras asked for the support of father Arnildo, their city parish priest. He not only lodged them in the parish house and provided them with food and clothing, but also read them the Bible from the Theology for Liberation's point of view, and made them meditate on the Third Chapter of the Book of the Exodus, which tells about the sufferings and the liberation of God's people, who were searching for the promised land. Those listening felt this was also their story. This is how this group decided to stay organized and struggle for the land.

Among the peasants who had been thrown out of the indigenous reserve there were those who wanted to occupy it once again. So one of the activities carried out by both father Arnildo and the Porto Alegre group was to convince those farmers that the Indians were right in claiming those lands because they belonged to them, and that there was plenty of land that could be legally distributed in the state of Rio Grande do Sul.

A whole process of organization, meetings and assemblies was carried out, where discussions took place and the people increased their political awareness.

In June 1978, about 30 of the expelled families, moved by desperation and – in a very individualistic manner – wanting to get ahead of the rest, decided to invade an area in the Sarandi *Fazenda*, in Rondinha, unaware that it was a forest reserve. They believed that it was enough to enter the area for it to be granted them. The police surrounded the place immediately and forced them to retreat. (24)

Informed of the process that was taking place in the camps installed at the roadside, the authorities started worrying and decided to offer those peasants lands in the colonization projects. The state government proposed to settle part of them in Bagé, in the southern part of the state. The federal government, on the other hand, outlined the possibility of doing the same thing in Mato Grosso, in what was known as the Terranova Project. One hundred and eighteen families went to Bagé and about 550 to Terranova. (25)

The rest of the families – about 500 – were still organized. Some time later – on August 1st – they decided to send a petition to governor Amaral de Souza, claiming the settlement in that state and announcing that if their demands were not met, they would occupy the Sarandi *Fazenda* once again. The governor asked for a 30-day time limit and demagogically declared that if their demands were not met he would personally accompany them in their occupation. Once the time limit ended and no answer was given, on September 7, at dawn, 110 families decided to occupy lands in Macali. The following day the military police arrived, (26) the peasants offered resistance, and the women placed themselves in the first row with their children. The police backed up, negotiations began with the governor, who was forced to honor his promise. He finally authorized the peasants to stay on that piece of land and withdrew the police force. (27)

Macali symbolizes the first conquest of the land in the middle of the military dictatorship. This victory encouraged new occupations in the region. Shortly after, Brilhante was occupied, and later Anoni.

The other sparks ignited in Santa Catarina (end of the 70s), Paraná (1980), São Paulo (1980), and Mato Grosso do Sul (from 1979 on).

Encruzilhada Natalino

The Encruzilhada Natalino camp (28) was the result of the previous experiences in the struggle. It started on December 8, 1980, when a settler called Natalio, who had been expelled from the

Indigenous Reserve of Nonoai, installed his tent at the fork of the roads leading to Ronda Alta, Sarandi and Passo Fundo, in the Ronda Alta Municipality of Rio Grande do Sul. More landless families then started coming from the whole region.

The camp – which started out with 50 families and ended up with 600, around 3000 people – was set up in a strategic place. The tents were spread out over 2 kilometers of highway.

The government tried unsuccessfully to deactivate the occupants, offering them work, but this was refused.

Taking this experience as a starting point, the families began organizing in groups, commissions and sectors. They even edited a news bulletin called *Sem Terra* that in time became the current MST newspaper. As symbol of their resistance they made a rustic cross that they carried during all their manifestations.

The campers started a technical survey of the latifundia existing in the nearest municipalities. They were thus able to show the government that the problems related to the land could be solved within their own region. In fact, 4000 hectares were on sale close to the camp.

On June 21, 1981, six months after the occupation of the land, Catholic bishop D. Pedro Casaldáliga, from São Félix de Araguaia (Mato Grosso), celebrated a mass as an expression of his solidarity with the campers. About 6000 people attended and the mass became known throughout the country, giving the struggle a national connotation.

Under this pressure, the federal government presented its proposal to transfer the families to the Roraima, Acre, Mato Grosso and Bahia colonization projects. But this second proposal was also refused. A month later, the peasants held another celebration, this time with Catholic bishop D. Tomás Balduíno, from Goiás Velho (Goiás), who denounced the misery of the settlers displaced to the Canamara colonization project in Mato Grosso. More than 10 000 people attended. According to D. Tomás, this event meant for the countryside what the São Paulo ABC strikes had represented for those city workers.

Since the government insisted on its proposal, the campers decided in an assembly that they would camp in front of the governmental building in Porto Alegre as a way to exert pressure. The Military Brigade prevented them from camping, but the governor received them. During the meeting they were informed that the army was going to surround the camp and those who were outside it would be unable to re-enter. They then went back as quickly as possible. The camp was taken over by troops commanded by colonel Curió – a specialist in repressing resistance of a popular nature – and it was declared Area of National Security. Curió said he would solve the problem in 15 days. To break down the campers' resistance he used different methods: he distributed food to the families but forced them to stand on line for many hours, during which time he would send out through loudspeakers information that would break down their mobilizing capacity; for example, an interview with the bishop from Porto Alegre in which he declared that landless peasants had no right to demand land in Rio Grande do Sul and that the government was not obliged to receive them; at other times the loudspeakers announced that those who did not accept being transferred to the colonization projects would receive no food.

Curió also put up a huge tent, where he showed slides of Acre, Roraima, Mato Grosso and Bahia, and proposed a commission to visit the area. Two planes came to pick up the peasants, and they were welcomed with a huge *assado* (grilled meat), but when the members of the group were washing their hands, water ran out. When the commission came back, most of its members declared that the project was impossible; the land was too sandy and water was scarce. Not a single family accepted moving to Bahia.

As a reaction to this refusal, violence against the campers grew. There was a continuous traffic of trucks that provoked a lot of dust and destroyed water sources. Horses were sent to trample their crops, creating panic. After this softening-up operation, they made another proposal for colonization, and were then able to divide the camp: 137 families accepted it.

Finally, they decided to put the camp under siege: it became like a concentration camp, where all visits were forbidden. This was denounced in the media and a huge manifestation was organized, with the participation of 137 priests from Rio Grande do Sul and Santa Catarina, members of the Lawyers' Association of Brazil, state and federal deputies. When they were prevented from entering the place, the campers took their cross and advanced with it, breaking down the military barrier. This changed the situation completely and the landless peasants recovered their hopes.

Once, when a camper tried to tune in on his radio, he discovered just by chance the station used by the intervening forces to communicate with Brasília. From that day on this camp was informed beforehand of all the movements planned by the enemy.

Another time, when Curió called the media to register the moment when he would give out candy, the children, who had been instructed by their parents and teachers, answered: "We don't want candy, we want land!"

On August 31st, a month after the beginning of his intervention, Curió had to retire. The resistance of the campers and the support of the people mentioned above were decisive in this victory.

Now free from the siege, the campers reorganized themselves and their ranks grew with families returning from Mato Grosso in disappointment.

Since the situation remained at a standstill and the authorities did not come forward with some kind of statement, they believed that the time had come to create something new for the struggle to go forward. In February 1982, during a meeting of the National Conference of Bishops, the campers proposed that the Church buy an area where the families could move on a provisional basis. This was accepted and the Church planned a national campaign to collect funds. The Lutheran Church also contributed. An area of 108 hectares was bought close to the Rio Passo Fundo Dam, in the Ronda Alta Municipality. This area was then named Nova Ronda Alta.

For more than a year and a half, the landless peasants insisted in their struggle. Before the elections for governor, they decided to discuss with the candidates their proposed solution for the land problem. In September 1983, the elected governor authorized the purchase of 1870 hectares for the final settlement of families from the Ronda Alta, Cruz Alta and Palmeira das Missões municipalities.

The struggle at Encruzilhada Natalino, in which peasants from eight municipalities of the region participated, was reflected in all Brazil, showing the need and the importance of agrarian reform.

Extension of the struggles to the rest of the country

These struggles for the land, in the Central-Southern region, extended rapidly all over the country. But there was still no national articulation.

First occupations

From the very first occupations, between 1979 and 1985, there was – according to João Pedro Stedile – a "romantic vision of production" (29): the worker of peasant background believed that it was enough to conquer the land and thus solve all his problems. When he received the land he thought only of himself and his family. His production habits were very individualistic. It was very hard for him to accept the possibility of collective work. His struggle was very personal, he did not think about the peasants and the working class as a whole. (30) Nor did he realize that the process of agricultural modernization the country was going through required the use of techniques that he "did not know much about." (31) The peasant tended to copy what he knew: family property in

37

the way of the "small owner." Production was devoted basically to survival, and only excess products went on to market. (32)

During this time, if there was some kind of cooperation it was limited to groups of mutual assistance and exchange of services. In some states, however, there were isolated experiences of agricultural cooperation: groups from the community or informal associations that had come up under the influence of the Catholic Church. (33)

But what did exist was resistance to a cooperative system, due to "the negative experiences of the traditional model existing in the country and characterized by huge agro-industrial concerns that developed a policy of economic exploitation of small farmers." (34)

This period ends with the creation of the Landless Movement in 1984, and their first congress the following year.

V – FOUNDATION

First National Meeting: foundation of the MST (January 21-24, 1984)

It was the Pastoral Commission of the Land to understand clearly that only a nation-wide movement could become an important political agent. (35)

At the beginning of this process, the idea was to create a regional movement. But later it became clear that a national movement would be the best way to strengthen the struggle for the land... and prevent it from being repressed or destroyed.

With this aim in mind, the First National Meeting of Landless Workers took place from the 21th to the 24nd of January 1984 (36), right in the middle of the struggle against the dictatorship. Popular leaders from several occupied lands participated: about 100 representatives from 13 states, among them – as I have already mentioned – numerous leaders from rural unions. (37)

The date of the First National Meeting is considered the date for the foundation of the MST.

The inclusion of the expression "rural workers" helps avoid the confusion between the movement of landless "rural workers," who occupy land to work it, and the movement of urban landless people, whose members occupy land to build their homes. This is really a popular movement for housing, and in many places it already exists under the more correct name Movement of Roofless People.

The Movement of Landless People is, therefore, a more popular abbreviation for the Movement of Landless Rural Workers, which also uses the initials MST. (38)

It was during this first meeting that its role was defined as that of an autonomous mass movement struggling for land, for agrarian reform. It is neither a union movement nor an ecclesiastic movement. It must not depend on the unions or the churches. It should rather be controlled by the workers themselves, so they can preserve its autonomy.

They insist on the fact that it must be a movement of class struggle, and not of bureaucratic negotiation at top levels. At that time, unions were accustomed to administrative action, they sent their demands to the National Institute for Colonization and Agrarian Reform (Incra), and in all congresses they requested agrarian reform – but that was all. That was the most common union activity. It was the MST that introduced mass struggle as a necessity. According to its leaders, this system of sending demands to the government with a list of signatures, assemblies etc., solved nothing at all. Experience had shown that it was the struggle of the masses – the only way to change the correlation of political forces in society – that made agrarian reform go forward. (39)

Work started in this First National Meeting to define future political action for the MST, and draw up the general objectives that would guide their performance. (40) The slogan "land for those who work it" – that had been used by the Pastoral Commission of the Land – was taken over by the MST. But from the very beginning this movement understood that agrarian reform cannot stop at the conquest of a piece of land. Rather, to implement it in an integral way there must also be a global transformation of society. For that reason, while struggling for the land to be controlled by those who work it, the MST also fights for a "just, equitable" society, "one that will put an end to capitalism." (41)

More precise objectives were also defined, such as the need to continue with the meetings for an exchange of experiences; the commitment of the unions with their struggles; the articulation of struggles in the countryside with those in the cities; solidarity with the struggle carried out by indigenous people as well as the defense of their right to land. (42) They also encouraged participation in the union movement and political parties, while trying to guarantee political autonomy for the Movement. One of the important objectives they discussed was the struggle for agrarian reform on land belonging to multinational corporations. "It was in this objective where the anti-imperialist character of the Movement appeared. It was not considered right for foreigners to own land in the country if there was just one landless Brazilian citizen left." (43)

Once these objectives were defined, the first meeting was followed by the intensification of the struggle for the land, mainly by means of occupations.

This increase in the struggles, together with the growth of the organization, required that municipal, regional and state commissions be organized. The better-organized states contributed to the formation of the MST in other states. (44)

VI – Important milestones in its history

Period of rapid growth (1985 – 1990)

First Congress (January 29 - 31, 1985)
The following year, a few days after Tancredo Neves was elected president, thus putting an end to long years of military

dictatorship, the MST held its First Congress in Curitiba, Paraná. There were 1500 delegates from 23 of Brazil's 26 states. The composition of the chair reflected the huge diversity of the forces committed to the struggle for agrarian reform. Besides the representatives from the MST state coordinating groups, there were Catholic bishops and archbishops, Lutheran pastors, representatives from the *Central Única dos Trabalhadores* (CUT) as well as from state government. (45)

Contrary to the position adopted by different sectors of the left, this Congress defined a political stand of not entering into a pact with the New Republic. (46) "Under the influence of both the PCB and the PCdoB (47) as well as other forces from the left, Contag and reformist unions believed that the National Plan for Agrarian Reform backed by the government would be implemented. For that reason, they considered that the peasant movement should adopt an attitude of cooperation with the government." (48) The MST, on the contrary, believed that the reform could not be subordinated to the good will of the new civil government, and it outlined the need to develop an overwhelming mass struggle that would exert pressure on its behalf. (49)

According to one of its leaders, João Pedro Stedile, at that time the Movement was weak, and should it have joined a larger and reformist force, the organization would have disappeared. (50)

One can thus understand the reason for the new slogan: "Occupation, the only solution," which substituted the one adopted by the First National Meeting: "Land for those who work it." Occupation became a strategic instrument until today.

Multiplication of occupations

Shortly after the First Congress, and when the democratic transitional period known as the New Republic had already started, important occupations began to multiply throughout the country.

In May of that year, west of Santa Catarina, the biggest series of occupations in just one region occurred. While president Sarney and the minister for agrarian reform participated in the Contag Congress with promises, in just one week the MST occupied 18 *fazendas*, moving 5000 families from 40 municipalities. "It was practically a revolution in that region. [...] The masses understood that they could not keep waiting for the government" and that they had to take advantage of the new democratic space for their mobilization and their struggle. (51)

The MST became a reference point for all those fighting for the land. Militants from other states began to approach it.

A step forward in association: small groups are formed as a starting point (52)

It is at this time that experiences at cooperation through association begin to multiply.

Through the Company for Technical Assistance and Rural Extension (Emater), the government stimulated them among small producers, while the MST did it among settlers.

The organization of production in the settlements started by forming small groups of 10 to 15 families for collective work.

It was an idealistic proposal inspired by religious motivations: the 12 apostles of the Gospel and the Christian communities at the base.

The pattern of the small groups of cooperation with no formal mediation for the implementation of different isolated or combined activities prevailed until 1989. What brought their members close together had different origins, rarely political ones. (53)

But these small groups, who were willing to work collectively, ended up in what some described as a "cooperation for survival," (54) because this method implied many limitations that were not evident in the beginning but that would become obstacles for the process of modernization in agriculture in the medium run.

First National Meeting of stttlers

In May 1986, the MST held its first discussion on how to organize the settlers and which forms of production to encourage. This took place during the First National Meeting of the Settlers, in Cascavel, Paraná, (55) with the participation of 76 settlements representing 11 states. This decision came about in a very particular context: due to the rapid growth in the number of settlements, especially in the state of São Paulo, where there was a progressive government, a minority current had come up at that time within the Movement that believed it would be convenient to form another popular movement outside the MST with those families who had already been settled, since they considered that if they had already obtained land, there was no reason for them to be tied to the Movement.

If the aim of the MST were only to conquer land, it would not be justified for those who had already conquered it to continue in its ranks. But the different experiences of agrarian reform implemented in other parts of the world show that it is not enough for the peasants to conquer the land; they must also have the conditions to work it: without machinery, seeds, credits, technical know-how to allow them to use the progress made in technological revolution; without outlets for their products – instead of becoming a space for freedom, the land becomes a nightmare and they end up selling it at very low prices, or simply abandoning it.

The struggle, therefore, does not end with the conquest of the land – that is only the first step. The rest of their objectives will be fully met when society will undergo a global transformation. Only if it fights against neoliberalism, which supports the important agro-industrial transnational corporations, will a radical agrarian reform come about. Meanwhile, they must plan and organize production to guarantee subsistence for the families already settled, and promote as far as possible "the socio-economic development of the peasants who are conquering the land." (56)

There are not only economic reasons, however; there are also ethical and political reasons: the fact that they have already conquered the land should not make these workers forget that there are still numerous other peasants who have not achieved this objective, and that those who now have better living conditions must show their solidarity with their brothers in the struggle.

At this meeting they adopted the strategic decision not to exclude those already settled from the MST. It is the settlements that help finance the Movement, allow for the liberation of cadres to work only on tasks of the organization etc. To consolidate this work, the National Commission, or Settlers' Sector, was set up and worked from 1986 to 1989.

Conquest of Procera (1986)

The most debated topic at that time was access to credit. The new government had put an end to the system of subsidized credits, (57) decreed by the military dictatorship to win the support of the peasants.

Without credits it was impossible to buy seeds and the necessary instruments to work the land. For that reason the MST organized its struggles to put pressure on the government so it would create a special line of credits for the settlements. In 1986 the Program for Special Credit for Agrarian Reform, better known as Procera, was implemented. (58)

Two agricultural credits were formed: the Procera Ceiling 1, a massive credit for all kinds of peasants, and the Procera Ceiling 2, only for cooperatives and associations, and double the amount of the first one. (59) It was a very convenient credit, not only because the member of the cooperative received twice the amount of the peasant who did not belong to the association, but also because it was granted on very long installments, thus allowing immediate investments in infrastructure, basic products and improvements in the housing conditions of settled families. (60) Its interest rate was very low and it included a 50% discount on both capital and interests.

Two other kinds of economic assistance were also granted: "credit for development," consisting in a small sum of money assigned to settled families so they could start their economic activities – they usually invested it in the purchase of work instruments and animals and, generally, these families ended up using it in a cooperated way. The other assistance was to build housing of at least 40 square meters. In general they made common purchases and the houses were built through mutual help. (61)

The problem presented by the credits granted by the state, in particular those for inputs for the year's agricultural work (seeds, fertilizer, machine-hours) was their linkage to specific technological packages, the so-called "green revolution."

The peasant had to prepare a project for his products, and the money he received was spent on inputs. He would pay it back with the year's crops. This system of short-term financing made the peasant depend on the purchase of the necessary seeds, and discouraged his own production.

This happened later with the Cooperative for Regional Marketing, Coanol, which ended up purchasing 100% of the seeds from the transnational corporations that have a monopoly over this trade. Today, the Cooperative is rectifying this attitude and it now produces 60% of its own seeds.

Different experiences at cooperation under study

There were two very different positions in the debate held on how to organize production: that of the agronomists, who wanted to organize it taking mainly into account the parameter of technical efficiency; and that of the priests, who insisted on the moral and human values of solidarity, fraternity etc. (62)

Some technicians (63) won over to the MST positions started to investigaate why the experiences at cooperation in Brazil had been unsuccessful. They also studied experiences in Nicarágua, Honduras, Chile, Peru, México and, more recently, those in Spain and Israel (64) and very specifically the case of Cuba's Cooperatives for Agricultural and Cattle-Raising Production (CPA).

The MST also established relations with Brazilian experts in this field, among them Clodomir Santos de Morais.

National MST Meeting and birth of large associations (1987)

The Third National MST Meeting was held in 1987. It drew guidelines to improve the settlements' organization. During this time the Movement expanded toward the Northeast and established contacts with large service associations (in machinery, marketing etc.) promoted by some progressive governments and by the Catholic Church. (65) Motivated by their example, which allowed for the accumulation of capital, several large associations came up in different parts of the country. (66) Collective work was not yet mentioned. They pursued the political representation of the settlers, giving them the services they needed, rather than collective production.

Even if these experiences were very limited, they nevertheless have the merit of having liberated the first cadres who were then able to devote their full time to the Movement.

Laboratory in Santos de Morais

Around that time, Clodomir Santos de Morais submitted a proposal for the organization of collective work in the countryside: it consisted of month-long laboratories for a practical rehearsal at cooperation.

These laboratories were conceived to make the peasant understand, during the 30-40 days of the experiment, that he had to give up rustic work methods that implied having him go personally through the whole process of production, and substitute them by the division of labor, as it is applied in industrial production. They aimed at teaching, through practical experience, the advantages of the division of labor. (67)

Throughout the laboratory they tried to fight against the vices that resulted from the rustic characteristics of peasant labor – individualism, personalism, spontaneousness, anarchism, immobility, accommodation, sectarianism or radicalism, sell-out attitudes, adventurism, self-reliance. (68)

These laboratories made an important contribution because they allowed the peasants to experiment in their own flesh that, alone and isolated, they could do nothing. On the other hand, if they joined the others, they could achieve much more, thus creating an awareness of the need to organize themselves.

Though the idea was good, its implementation was not always positive. Often these laboratories did not respect local dynamics, the peasant rhythm, and the life history of the people, cultural aspects... Once the group was formed – between 50 and 100 families already camped and willing to organize themselves – it was stipulated that 40 days later the cooperative had to come into existence. But the peasants usually mature at a much slower pace and the groups of agricultural cooperation tend to emerge little by little, according to the affinities that are created in the camps.

Training Courses Integrated into Production (FIP)

As soon as the laboratories were discarded because of these deficiencies, courses that lasted between 15 and 20 days were organized in the camps – they were known as *Cursos de Formação Integrada à Produção* (Training Courses Integrated into Production, FIP). The peasants worked and studied at the same time. Class hours depended on the needs of production. The contents were both political and technical. (69)

The thrust given by the MST to the formation of cooperatives at that time was intensified – according to Álvaro de la Torre – by the existence of public assistance, like the Procera, which stimulated association, and by the way in which the MST appraised people according to their willingness to become members of a cooperative.

Those willing to do so were considered revolutionary, and the rest was treated with contempt. (70)

Campaign from the right against the settlements – accent on production

Within the context of a political debate around agrarian reform in the new Constitution they were drafting (71), and in view of the increasing number of MST settlements all over the country, the landowners decided to organize their resistance and fight with all their weapons. Besides repression – which included the murder of many union leaders in the struggle for the land – they tried to convince public opinion that they had to preserve the right to property over the land. The struggle of these large landowners during the constitutional process was aimed at guaranteeing the absolute right of property, while accepting that only uncultivated land, called unproductive land, could be disappropriated.

This kind of attack made the MST become more interested in the efficiency of production within the settlements. It was not enough to form an association to carry out collective work – they also had to prove that agrarian reform was a viable thing and that it could solve many of the existing social problems. (72)

This led to an internal discussion to discover the best way to produce on a large scale, market the products and create agro-industries. They believed that production must lower its costs and increase its quality. This process made the peasants understand that they would be able to resist capitalism in the countryside only if they left rustic agriculture behind and updated their social relations of production. Otherwise, they would be swallowed up by the system and expelled once again to the outskirts of the large cities.

Fifth National Meeting

The Fifth National Meeting was held in 1989, in an atmosphere of intense political fervor – the mass movement in

48

general was growing, both the CUT and the PT were consolidating, and it was even believed that Lula would win the 1989 presidential elections. (73)

The new slogan, "Occupy, resist, produce," was thus born at this meeting. The new element was "produce." They also strongly believed that the settlements had to generate a new type of society, that production had to be organized in a different way, drawing up their own model for agriculture. They were also convinced of the importance that the leader of the Workers' Party, Lula, be elected president, so the country could begin to change. (74)

COLLOR DE MELO'S OFFENSIVE AGAINST THE MST

Second MST National Congress

The Second MST National Congress was held in Brasília in 1990, shortly after Lula's defeat and the arrival of Collor de Melo as the new president. It was not just an electoral defeat, it was also a political and moral defeat for the working class as a whole. (75) It put an end to 10 years of growth in Brazil's mass movement. It affected the militants' morale and in the specific case of the MST, it affected its hopes of implementing a deep and quick agrarian reform. The Movement then entered into one of its worse periods.

The first measure of the new government was to repress it. Federal police invaded its state headquarters, took away its documents and backed legislative trials against it, determined to put an end to the MST. (76)

Though the slogan "Occupy, resist, produce" was still used from 1989 to 1994, the accent was put on the word "resist." The Movement realized that the struggle would be very hard, that the development attained until then was not enough to stop Collor's offensive, and that it was therefore necessary to strengthen the organic aspects of the Movement as well as the settlements. The MST thus attempted to unite its more active members into militant nuclei and to encourage Cooperatives for Agricultural and Cattle-Raising Production as the strongest political and economic points of resistance. (77)

There were long discussions over the Cooperative System of the Settlers (SCA) that gave place to the idea of creating the Confederation of Agrarian Reform Cooperatives in Brazil (Concrab) (78).

The first cooperatives for production and their search for a new model

A few months after the Second MST Congress, Rio Grande do Sul witnessed the appearance of the first Cooperatives for Agricultural and Cattle-Raising Production (CPAs). (79)

One of the reasons for this was that at that time changes were being made into the Magna Carta. Before passing the new Constitution in 1988, the cooperatives were under the control of both Incra and the State Cooperative Organization. That is why the MST practically did not speak about cooperatives, and it started to do so only when the new legislation recognized the autonomy of these bodies, relieving Incra from its power to intervene in them.

The Movement considers they have to recover the original contents of the cooperative experience. It believes the idea comes from the European working class at the end of the 19th century, and that the bourgeoisie took it over and then deformed it. That explains why the cooperatives it tries to create are different from capitalist ones, since they are made up exclusively of small producers and their families – in other words, only of workers – and try to give priority to the needs of their associates instead of the growth of the enterprise and the excluding logic this objective imposes. (80)

The system of cooperation supported by the MST aims at "developing a process of cooperation in the countryside, respecting its different forms." (81) It believes it must "organize the settlers and small peasants in groups of families or groups of production" (82) and that regional differences must be respected, and a new technological model sought. (83)

Creation of the Settlers System of Cooperation (1990)

The creation of the Settlers' System of Cooperation (SCA) (84) begins in 1990. The system takes into account the results of the studies carried out to build "new ways of productive life in the countryside." They believe that the CPAs are a "superior stage of collective organization of the land" (85) but that does not mean they should ignore other forms of production. They consider, therefore, that the system must include both individual peasants and associations, collective groups, CPAs and the Regional Marketing Cooperatives that had emerged to allow the CPAs to market their products under better conditions.

Intention of creating its own credit system

One of the measures adopted by Collor de Melo's government to prevent any progress for agrarian reform in the country was to totally dismantle the credits and public policies for agriculture. The MST then understood the need to guarantee that the settlers have permanent credits, and it came up with the creation of its own mechanisms for credits. The initial idea was to create "a large central credit cooperative" to capture resources from the government, foreign entities, the World Bank and other financial bodies. After two years' discussion with experts on the matter, they came to the conclusion that the project was not possible. Since the law required first to operate on a municipal level and then on the central one, this would have meant only tens of small credit cooperatives – in the beginning it would have implied only an increase in administrative expenses, without guaranteeing the immediate credits they so badly needed. (86)

Central Offices of General Cooperatives

Finally, they came to the conclusion that the solution to the credit problem was not the creation of credit cooperatives, but of Central Offices of Agricultural Cooperatives (CCA) (87) that would join in the same body the marketing cooperatives, the different forms of agricultural cooperation, the associations and even the cooperatives of small farmers. (88)

When these central offices were conceived, they determined their own economic aims, but later it became evident that material conditions did not exist for this to be possible. They were unable, for example, to place themselves on the market. In fact, the Central Offices of these Cooperatives became only the political articulation of the settlers, an instrument for the implementation of the MST guidelines for cooperation, and they ended up being a good instrument of political representation before the state. (89)

They were in charge of coordinating the CPAs' sales and purchases, organizing transportation of agricultural products and purchasing the machinery and other equipment that a CPA was unable to obtain all by itself. (90)

Creation of Concrab (1992)

The idea was for these cooperatives to organize at a state level and become part of a National Confederation.

By May 1992 there were four state central cooperatives: Rio Grande do Sul, Santa Catarina, Paraná and Espírito Santo, so they created the Confederation of Agricultural Cooperatives for Agrarian Reform in Brazil (Concrab) led by the MST (91) and later, through the Cooperative Settlers' System, an effort was made so the idea of these central cooperatives would be known in the other states. (92) Today there are nine of them, the five new ones being São Paulo, Bahia, Parnambuco, Ceará and Maranhão.

Period of recovery and advance

Itamar Franco's government favors struggle for the land (1992-1994)

Collor's dismissal was a political victory and the arrival of Itamar Franco's government a relief for the MST, because it opened up a period similar to that of the New Republic, though evidently not as progressive as far as social victories was concerned. The government negotiated with the MST through the minister of labor (93), who opened up spaces for the Movement to be considered a political representative. And then, for the first time, a president officially received a delegation of that organization. (94)

National Seminar on cooperation (end 1994)

At the end of 1994 a national seminar was held on "The Future of Cooperation within the MST." They came to the conclusion that though the Cooperatives for Agricultural and Cattle-Raising Production are the best means to organize work, what really allows massive cooperation in settlements are non-productive activities, such as service cooperatives.

In the second half of the 90s, Service Cooperatives became very numerous at the regional level. They organized the process of trading production, inputs and consumer goods. They also lent technical assistance and training, and applied different planning methods at the municipal or micro-regional levels. (95)

On the other hand, this seminar verified that what determines the viability of cooperation in production is not the size of the lot of land, but its location, the technological model used, the amount of capital available, and the possibilities of the market. They also came to the conclusion that the introduction of agro-industry was a strategic aspect for the economic development of the settlements, for it integrated youth and added value to production. Finally, they believed that there would be no autonomous development for the settlements without a state intervention controlled and guided by the working class, where the state would have to play an inductive role in the cooperatives through an adequate credit, technical assistance and research system, eliminating the possibility of a "primitive accumulation" of capital through that method.

Foundation of Iterra (1995)

In January 1995 the Instituto Técnico de Capacitação e Investigação de Reforma Agrária (Technical Institute for Training and Research on Agrarian Reform, Iterra,) was founded in Veranópolis, Rio Grande do Sul. Its first task was to take over the Technical Course on Cooperative Management (TAC), and later it decided to organize a teachers' course aimed at forming professors. It was named the Josué de Castro School.

Third MST Congress (1995)

The Third MST Congress was held in July 1995 in Brasília, several months after Fernando Henrique Cardoso became president of the Republic. There were about 5000 delegates from the whole country.

One of its conclusions was the need to fight against that neoliberal government because it came head on in contradiction with the need to develop agrarian reform.

They also understood that for agrarian reform to go forward, all of society must embrace it as a legitimate struggle of landless people poor peasants, and also as the origin of positive consequences for that very society. The people had to understand that the development of the country as a whole would be possible only if the countryside was developed. Moving the poor to the cities would mean a living hell for all. This was summed up in the slogan: *"Agrarian reform is everyone's struggle."*

On the other hand, that Congress also proved that it was possible to hold successful mass meetings. It never foresaw that these meetings would analyze subjects in depth. Agrarian reform, for example, could not be discussed there – that kind of discussion should be carried out in previous smaller meetings, since the MST wants to create spaces for meetings, brotherhood and the consolidation of the protagonists of this struggle for the land throughout the country. The most valuable aspect of these meetings is the force emanating from the fact of being together and sharing experiences, learning from each other.

From that moment on, the different states held mass meetings with more than 1000 people. In the past they had had a limited amount of delegates, ranging from 250 to 300. (97)

It is during this congress that the MST agrarian program was adopted, after a long ideological debate carried out from 1993 to 1995.

This program "represents a proposal for the reorganization of the countryside in Brazil. It tries to make landholding and knowledge more democratic. For the first time it talks about access to education and school organization as part of an agrarian program, an agrarian reform. In the past, according to the classic attitude, a program for agrarian reform only talked about the distribution of land. For the MST it is as important to distribute land as it is to distribute knowledge, [agrarian reform is part of] a larger process for the development of the countryside that is based on the development of the people, so they can be happier and more educated even if they live in the middle of a field." (98)

The Congress also incorporated the idea of agro-industry, because it broke with the tradition of being a movement of simple peasants who think only of agriculture. "We cannot stop and produce only raw materials and allow the capitalists to enrich themselves at our expense" – declares João Pedro Stedile. "We have to go a step further: we ourselves must transform the raw material the land produces, so the agro-industrial multinational corporations will not exploit us; put added value on them and be able to sell the product at lower prices, yet increasing our access to the mass market of the city." (99)

The Fernando Henrique Cardoso Administration and its tactics (1994-1998)

During its first years in power, the Fernando Henrique Cardoso Administration did not use uniform tactics against the MST. At first it tried to ignore it. This tactics was involuntarily defeated by the Corumbiara massacre in August 1995 (100), which revealed to the world the existence of the agrarian problem in Brazil; later, by the organization of a huge congress in Brasília. The Third National Congress gathered the impressive figure of 5000 delegates: it was impossible to deny the existence and strength of a movement capable of mobilizing so many people. (101)

Once this tactics failed, the government then tried to co-opt the Movement, naming Francisco Graziano, a well-known person in the academic world, president of Incra. While this character visited MST camps and acted out a "honeymoon" with them, the Movement prepared a huge wave of land occupations throughout the country, which took place in mid-1996. (102)

Understanding that this new tactics did not work either, the government then decided to use isolation: it did not negotiate. To oppose this attitude, the MST organized the big march on Brasília in April 1997, and due to its massive and combative contents it shook all of Brazil. After this event, violence prevailed. (103)

Thus came into action the three aspects of the classic tactics of the dominating classes against a growing popular movement: first, the attempt at co-option, "handing out a few crumbs or flattering conceited, individualistic or ideologically-weak leaders"; (104) second, the effort to divide the mass movement; and third, repression. If co-option or division don't work, try repression. "The bourgeoisie has always acted this way in class struggle. The MST has to be ready for it", declares João Pedro Stedile. (105)

CRISIS RESULTING FROM THE IMPLEMENTATION OF THE AMERICAN MODEL TO THE BRAZILIAN COUNTRYSIDE

According to Stedile (106), it was during Cardoso's second mandate that the MST started to understand all the consequences the so-called "North-American agricultural model" would have for small farmers and for the efforts at rural development they were attempting in the settlements. This model stimulated the development of large highly mechanized *fazendas* – with the consequent reduction in the work force – totally integrated in the market.

As soon as the large strategic state companies – electricity, telephone, minerals – became private, Cardoso turned to agriculture in full.

This model is based on a large internationalization of the economy. Domestic markets are supplied by imported products. "In the past, practically no agricultural products were imported; we only imported a little wheat from Argentina, but 90% was produced in the country. Today we spend 5 billion dollars a year in food for the domestic market, when practically all these products could grow in Brazil."

The general characteristics of this model are:

A domestic market under the control of large companies and internationalized prices

"First, the establishment of a national agricultural market under the control of large companies. In the past, each region of Brazil had its own markets and its own prices. The price of corn in one state was different from that in another state: that of Chapecó was different from that of Fortaleza, because the price was defined by the cost of production in the region. This does not work today, there is only one market – in other words, the same company supplies Chapecó, Porto Velho, Fortaleza, and Recife. But things do not stop there. Since many of these companies are multinational corporations, what happens is that the prices also become prices of the international market. The prices of agricultural products are no longer formed according to the logic of internal economy. This is the big change that has occurred. Today, corn has the same price in Chapecó and Fortaleza. On the other hand, if there is no corn in Fortaleza, they don't look for it in Rio Grande do Sul, they bring it in from Canadá, Argentina. Three multinational corporations control today almost 90% of the corn trade in Brazil: Cargill, Dupont and Burg Borns." (107)

Oligopolization of agro-industries

Second: a process of oligopolization and denationalization of agro-industries.

"From an economic point of view, this is nonsense because due to Brazil's dimensions, they could install agro-industries in each small city. This would generate more employment and a more homogeneous process of development. But on the contrary, what happened during these last four years was a process of very violent oligopolization in these agro-industries. For example, practically three companies control the milk market in Brazil: Nestlé, Glória (a US company) and Parmalat. All small producers as well as our cooperatives are forced to sell them the milk they produce. That is why the price of milk is so low for the producer and so high for the consumer: milk is priced according to the international market. In Brazil you pay for milk the same price as in Italy, but the Brazilian producer is paid very little. Parmalat pays 20 cents of a *real* per liter to the farmer, and sells the milk at 1 *real* – five times the original price. In Italy, on the contrary, milk is paid 50 cents a liter. The margin of benefits for these industries there is much lower. There are hundreds of them. Each city has one.

"This very low price paid to Brazil's milk producers prevents them from leaving poverty behind. They must produce 5 liters of milk to buy a can of Coca-Cola. Great result for this model!" (108)

Reduction of the role of the public sector in agriculture

Third, the reduction of the role of the public sector in agriculture. "It is well-known that agriculture as an economic activity requires in all countries of the world, and especially in capitalist countries, the support of the state to be able to continue its activity. Many aspects of agriculture do not depend on human will, but on nature, climate etc. That is why the state has to protect it in different ways; it must organize agricultural activity because it is so atomized that it cannot depend on each individual farmer's wishes. A component of classic capitalist economic policy is that the state must organize storage; grant credits and technical assistance for production; control prices; finance research in the agricultural and cattle-raising fields. (109)

"But today, with the new model, the Brazilian state is abandoning agriculture. It does not control storage, or prices, nor does it grant credits. During the military dictatorship, the Banco do Brasil, a public bank, gave about 18 billion dollars a year for agriculture, while in the year 2000 only 3 billion dollars were assigned. So that after 30 years and in spite of the increase in production, public funds earmarked for agricultural loans shrank six times." (110)

Agricultural Technological Pattern

"The fourth characteristic of this model is that now we are going into a new revolution – that of biotechnology. But this revolution has fallen under the monopoly of the large transnational corporations. They guide and monopolize seed control, thus being able to impose on the farmers a new technological pattern.

"Monsanto, for example, besides what it means to produce different varieties of transgenic soy (111), tries to force every farmer who buys this seed to purchase at the same time the herbicide or insecticide only they produce and have prepared for this kind of seed. The benefits for this corporation are not in the seeds but in the herbicide or insecticide specifically good for that seed. If the farmer buys the seeds he must also buy the poison produced by Monsanto.

"At present, Brazil is facing a serious problem with seed monopolization. At the time of the military dictatorship, it was Embrapa (112) that produced seeds – it was a public company and all the new varieties of seeds it discovered were available to everyone. All those who wanted to purchase them could do so, at low prices, because the state subsidized them. Now, only four years later, Monsanto and Cargill already control 65% of all wheat seeds in Brazil: this product is going down the same road as soy.

"This is in fact a model that concentrates benefits and the property of land, and people understand this clearly. Five years ago all of Brazil's cotton production was in the hands of small farmers, in São Paulo as well as in North of Paraná and the Northeast. This new policy transferred cotton production to Mato Grosso and now there are enormous extensions of highly mechanized large *fazendas*. The biggest of them all, with an area of 100 000 hectares totally devoted to cotton, employs up to 20 harvesters. Everything is mechanized; and the same happens with wheat, soy and rice." (113)

Today, the government's agricultural policies have intensified the crisis suffered by small farmers and have struck the MST a hard blow.

The Movement is now the object of a huge offensive by the government, which is determined to implement the neo-liberal agro-exporting model at any price. It has cut credits for cooperatives (114); now not only are there fewer credits, but they all come from a single fund – this is a method to throw part of the peasants against the other, stimulating division between those who belong to the MST and other small farmers.

These measures, together with the crisis in small agriculture as a result of the model for agricultural exports, have dealt a hard blow to the MST. Frustration and depression have pervaded the settlers, because they now see further and further away on the horizon the possibility of revenues that would allow them to improve significantly their living conditions through a kind of agriculture alternative to the official model.

The leaders are getting their base ready for a period of resistance: they must not live off the hope of getting credits and outside assistance, but rather see how they continue forward with their own resources.

But not only does the government cut their resources, it also applies other tactics to weaken the Movement. It has applied a formula to discourage mobilization and land occupation. It knows that it is through this method that the MST has been able to settle so many people and that this has given it great strength, because it has shown its members at the base that if they organize themselves and fight, they can achieve their objectives. That is why the government announced it would give land to all those who would apply by mail during a 120-day time limit. The MST replied transforming this proposal into a boomerang. Instead of fighting against those peasants who would apply on an individual basis because they lacked awareness – and this was precisely the idea the government had in mind – the tactics applied was that the farmers should appear massively at the post offices. All families camped in one specific place – let us recall that the MST organizes massive camps that go from 1000 to 1500 people from different municipalities – came to ask for their applications forms, but since the post offices were not prepared for a massive show up, they didn't have enough for so many people. The actions have unveiled the government's demagogy: time limits expire, yet the land is not given out.

On the other hand, the MST has come to an agreement with other important peasant organizations in the country: Movement of Small Farmers (MPA), Movement of People Affected by Dams (MAB) (115), and Movement of Rural Women, together with sectors of the National Confederation of Workers in Agriculture (Contag), to negotiate together, so the government will be unable to apply different policies in order to favor one movement in detriment of the others.

The MST is struggling at the same time together with peasant movements from different parts of the world (116), against transgenic productions and the use of agrotoxic products. And it is one of the movements heading the struggle against NAFTA in Latin America.

The government's campaign in the media

But not only does the government attempt to drown the Movement economically, it also tries to destroy its image in the media, wishing to throw public opinion against it and confuse its social base, through a systematic campaign of disinformation. The newspapers print the official speech but hide police violence against the MST.

"Mass media are very strong and they are on top of us at all hours of the day looking for a mistake, anything, and even making up lies to demoralize the Movement," says Marcelo Batista, a cadre of the MST. (117)

Recently, the government and the media not only attack a settlement or a concrete action carried out by the MST, they also cruelly undermine its honesty and principles.

At the end of the year 2000, "the lies became so serious that they were the object of repudiation by bodies such as the National Conference of Bishops of Brazil (CNBB), the Order of Lawyers of Brazil (OAB), and the National Council of Christian Churches (Conic)." (118)

In November 2000, members of Parliament and mayors belonging to the Workers' Party published a manifesto denouncing the campaign of the government against the Movement. They said, "[…] the government decided to unleash a meticulously articulated action against the MST. Updating old accusations, financing trips for journalists willing to sell themselves for a few cents, it put in the minds of public opinion the image of a movement whose main reason for existing was to deviate the course of public funds. With an unusual agility, the Federal Police [broke into] farmers' homes, [while] the [officialist] rural parliamentarians had already prepared a report, and numerous investigations [...] were being launched against its leaders throughout the whole country. [...]." (119)

"The evident aim of this strategic operation was to eliminate the MST, just as the Peasant Leagues had been eliminated during the first few months of the military regime." (120)

In spite of this, a survey of opinion of the year 2000 revealed that 56% of all Brazilians supported the struggle of the MST, while only 14% approved the policies of the Cardoso Administration. (121)

This systematic campaign, however, started having negative effects at the base because many of the MST members were not sufficiently prepared ideologically for the great offensive that had hit them. In this dangerous situation, the leadership of the Movement reacted very energetically, deciding to make huge efforts to train their militants, so they in turn would be able to prepare their families better and head off the offensive. From the year 2001 there has been a massive campaign for the training of cadres all over the country, so they can also prepare their people at the base to face this difficult situation. (122)

In spite of all these efforts to stop it, the MST has been able to consolidate itself as the main national reference point for the struggle against neoliberalism.

NOTES

1. Ultabs: *União de Lavradores e Trabalhadores Agrícolas do Brasil* (Unions of Peasants and Agricultural Workers of Brazil).
2. Master: *Movimento dos Agricultores Sem Terra* (Movement of Landless Farmers).

3. Getúlio Vargas, 1930-1945.
4. Partner: he who rents someone else's land to work it.
5. Farmer who must share half his crop with the owner of the land.
6. Bernardo Mançano Fernandes, *A Formação do MST no Brasil*, Editora Vozes, Petrópolis, 2000, p. 33.
7. João Pedro Stedile and Frei Sérgio, *La Lucha por la Tierra en el Brasil*, MST, São Paulo, 1999, p. 14.
8. B. Mançano Fernandes, *A Formação do MST...* op. cit. , p. 34.
9. J. P. Stedile and Frei Sérgio, *La Lucha por la Tierra...*, op. cit., op. 14-15.
10. Op. cit., pp. 14-15.
11. Op cit., p. 15.
12. The Statute for the Land was a federal law that wanted to regulate the process of occupation of property and establish legal rules for agrarian reform. It defined the juridical concept of the social function of the land. It also made a definition of categories that did not exist in the past: *minifúndio e latifúndio*, concepts that took into account the ideas of exploitation and extension. (Alberto Martínez, Letter to Marta Harnecker, December 2, 2001).
13. B. Mançano Fernandes, *A Formação do MST...*, op. cit., p. 43.
14. J. P. Stedile and B. M. Fernandes, *Brava gente, la trayectoria del MST y de la lucha por la tierra en Brasil,* Ed. Barbarroja, Argentina, 2000, p. 16; Brazilian edition: Editorial F. Perseu Abramo, maio 1996, p. 16.
15. J. P. Stedile and Frei Sérgio, *La Lucha por la Tierra...*, op. cit., p. 15.
16. J. P. Stedile and B. Mançano Fernandes, *Brava gente...*, op. cit., p. 17; Braz. Edition, p. 17.
17. J. P. Stedile and Frei Sérgio, *La Lucha por la Tierra...*, op. cit., p. 17.
18. Ibidem.
19. A large part of the information I give here was made available by Frei Flávio Vivian, of the Maria Elizabeth settlement in the Tupan Silatan Municipality, Rio Grande do Sul, Interview by Marta Harnecker, May 2001.
20. J. P. Stedile, Os Sem Terra, *Teoria & Debate* magazine, N° 9, Jan.-Mar. 1990, p. 6.
21. Op. cit., p. 7.
22. "She was the important element responsible for the birth of the Landless Movement, because she knew everything and everyone...", op. cit., p. 8.

23. Movement for the Union of Christian Churches.
24. Up to here, information from João Pedro Stedile (letter to Marta Harnecker, March 24, 2001).
25. B. Mançano Fernandes, *A Formação do MST*..., op. cit., p. 51.
26. In the state of Rio Grande do Sul it is called "military brigade."
27. B. Mançano Fernandes, *A Formação do MST*..., op. cit., p. 53.
28. On this subject, see B. Mançano Fernandes, op. cit., pp. 54-61.
29. J. P. Stedile and B. Mançano Fernandes, *Brava Gente*..., p. cit., p. 95.
30. Concrab, *Sistema Cooperativista dos Assentados*, Caderno de Cooperação Agrícola N° 5, 2nd edition, June 1998, p. 28.
31. J. P. Stedile and B. Mançano Fernandes, *Brava Gente*..., op. cit., p. 95; Braz. Ed. Pp. 50-51.
32. Concrab, *Sistema Cooperativista dos*..., op. cit., p. 28.
33. Op cit., p. 29.
34. Concrab, *A Evolução da Concepção de Cooperação Agrícola do MST (1989-1999)*, Caderno de Cooperação Agrícola N° 8, August 1999, p. 6
35. B. Mançano Fernandes, *A Formação do MST*..., op. cit., pp. 75-76.
36. In the Diocesan Training Center in Cascavel, Paraná.
37. J. P. Stedile, *Os Sem Terra*, op cit., p. 7.
38. The initials *MST* (Movimento Sem Terra) were first used in the Ronda Alta camp in 1983, when the leaders of Encruzilhada Natalino created a commission to organize protests, when they discovered a new governmental project to build 25 hydroelectric plants on the Uruguai river, at the frontier between Santa Catarina and Rio Grande do Sul.
39. J. P. Stedile and B. Mançano Fernandes, *Brava Gente*..., op. cit., p. 56; Braz. Edit., p. 50.
40. B. Mançano Fernandes, *A Formação do MST*..., op. cit., p. 83.
41. MST, *Construindo o Caminho*, op. cit., p. 44. See here the five principles mentioned in Cascavel.
42. B. Mançano Fernandes, *A Formação do MST*..., op. cit., p. 83.
43. J. P. Stedile and B. Mançano Fernandes, *Brava Gente*..., op. cit., pp. 56-57; Braz. Edit., pp. 50-51.
44. B. Mançano Fernandes, *A Formação do MST*..., op. cit., p. 84.
45. Op cit., p. 88.

46. Period of democratic transition that begins at the end of the military dictatorship and when José Sarney becomes president (1985-1990), after the death of Tancredo Neves.

47. Communist Party of Brazil.

48. Stedile, *Os Sem Terra*, op. cit., p. 7.

49. "[...] We do not refuse to discuss with the New Republic, there were even bonds of friendship with the comrades from ABRA. [We] stayed 10 or 12 days in Brasília [...] contributing to the plan. We made [many] suggestions within the plan. Now we still believe that Agrarian Reform will be able to come out of this paper only if it is the result of the mobilization of our people, a mass movement. And we go on articulating the bases" [Stedile, *Os Sem Terra.*, op. cit., p. 7].

50. J. P. Stedile and B. Mançano Fernandes, *Brava Gente...*, op. cit., p. 58; Braz. Edit., p. 52.

51. Op. cit., p. 58; Braz. Edit., pp. 52-53.

52. On this subject see Concrab, *Sistema Cooperativista...*, op. cit., pp. 29-30.

53. Concrab, *A Evolução da Concepção...*, op. cit., p. 28.

54. Frei Sérgio Antonio Gorgen and João Pedro Stedile, *Assentamentos...*, op. cit., p. 151.

55. J. P. Stedile and B. Mançano Fernandes, *Brava Gente...*, op. cit., p. 104; Braz. Edit., p. 88.

56. J. P. Stedile and Frei Sérgio, *La Lucha por la Tierra...*, op. cit., p. 47.

57. A sort of donation or subsidy given the farmer with demagogic ends.

58. This form of credit was eliminated by Fernando Henrique Cardoso's government in the year 2000. From that date on the settlers have to fight for resources with the small farmers, who have a new kind of credit called PRONAF (National Program for the Enhancement of Family Agriculture). The program for technical assistance to the settlements (LUMIAR), created in 1997, was also eliminated.

59. In fact, once this credit disappeared, there was also a reduction in the interest to form cooperatives (Álvaro de la Torre, Interview by Marta Harnecker, May 2001). No one is against encouraging the constitution of cooperatives through credit; what is considered negative within

the MST is that it turns out to be the main motivation for many farmers to accept this system.

60. J. P. Stedile and Frei Sérgio, *La Lucha por la Tierra...*, op. cit., p. 49.
61. Norberto Martínez, Interview by Marta Harnecker, São Paulo, May 20, 2001.
62. Concrab, *Sistema Coooperativista dos...*, op.cit., p. 30.
63. That was the case for Lino de David, from Rio Grande do Sul, who later organized the Center for Alternative Agricultural and Cattle-Raising Techniques (CETAP), of Geraldo Garcia and Norbert Hesselen, among others. J. P. Stedile and B. Mançano Fernandes, *Brava Gente...*, op. cit., p. 114; Braz. Edit., p. 97.
64. Op. cit., p. 114; Braz. Edit., pp. 97-98.,
65. It is interesting to note that in the Nordeste and the North there is more knowledge about cooperation than in other regions of the country; that is the reason why Incra, when it designs settlements, does not divide the land into individual lots.
66. Concrab, *Sistema Cooperativista dos...*, op. cit., p. 30.
67. Mário Schons, Interview by Marta Harnecker, Chapecó, May 8, 2001.
68. Clodomir S. de Morais, *Elementos sobre a Teoria da Organização no Campo*, Movement of Rural Landless Workers, August 1986, pp. 27-39.
69. Norberto Martínez, Interview by Marta Harnecker, op. cit.
70. Álvaro de la Torre, Interview by Marta Harnecker, Porto Alegre, May 2001.
71. It was approved on October 5, 1998.
72. Frei Sérgio, Antonio Gorgen and J. P. Stedile, *Assentamentos*, op. cit., p. 150.
73. J. P. Stedile and B. Mançano Fernandes, *Brava Gente...*, op. cit., p. 53; Braz. Edit., op. 167.
74. Ibidem.
75. J. P. Stedile and B. Mançano Fernandes, *Brava Gente...*, op. cit., pp. 59-60; Braz. Edit. Pp. 53-54.
76. Op. cit., p. 60; Braz. Edit., p. 54.
77. Concrab, *A Evolução da Concepção de Cooperação...*, op. cit., pp. 6-7.

78. J. P. Stedile and B. Mançano Fernandes, *Brava Gente...*, op. cit., p. 60; Braz. Edit., p. 54.

79. Copanor (Nova Ramada Agricultural and Cattle-Raising Cooperative) created after the laboratory in Santos de Morais, with 73 associates; Cooptil (Cooperative for Production Integration Work, Ltd.), created in October 1989 in the Bagé (Hulha Negra) Municipality with 41 associates, and Cooptar.

80. B. Mançano Fernandes gives a comparative picture in his book *A Formação do MST no Brasil*, p. 230. See also the Concrab publication: Sistema Cooperativista dos Assentados, Caderno de Cooperação Agrícola N° 5, 2nd edition, June 1998, pp. 9-11.

81. Ibidem.

82. B. Maçano Fernandes, *A Formação do MST...*, op. cit., p. 11.

83. Ibidem.

84. Putting an end to a discussion first started in 1989.

85. Concrab, *Sistema Cooperativista dos...*, op. cit., p. 31.

86. J. P. Stedile and B. Mançano Fernandes, *Brava Gente...*, op. cit., p. 121; Braz. Edit., p. 104.

87. The idea was to form a central office for cooperation, and to make it legal it had to be named cooperative.

88. J. P. Stedile and B. Mançano Fernandes, *Brava Gente...*, op. cit., pp. 120-121; Braz. Edit., pp. 104.105.

89. Norberto Martínez, Interview by Marta Harnecker, op. cit.

90. Concrab, *A Evolução da Concepção de Cooperação...*, op. cit., p. 10.

91. R. Salete Caldart, *Pedagogia do Movimento Sem Terra*, Editora Vozes, Petrópolis, Rio de Janeiro, 2000, p. 91.

92. J. P. Stedile and B. Mançano Fernandes, *Brava Gente...*, op. cit., p. 122; Braz. Edit., p. 105.

93. Walter Barelli.

94. J. P. Stedile and B. Mançano Fernandes, *Brava Gente...*, op. cit., pp. 85-86; Braz. Edit., pp. 70-71.

95. B. Mançano Fernandes, *A Formação do MST...*, op. cit., p. 233.

96. J. P. Stedile and B. Mançano Fernandes, *Brava Gente...*, op. cit., p. 61; Braz. Edit., p. 55.

97. Op. cit., p. 62; Braz. Edit., p. 56.

98. Op. cit., pp. 92-93; Braz. Edit., pp. 76-77.

99. Op. cit., p. 93; Braz. Edit., p. 77.

100. At dawn on August 9, 1995, about 187 military police obeyed orders to expel 500 landless families from the Santa Elina *Fazenda*, in Corumbiara (Rondonia). This turned into a bloody massacre in which the peasants were "executed, tortured, humiliated. There were shots, running, deformed faces, tears. Deaths. Ten workers and two policemen dead." (MST on Line, May 2001).

101. J. P. Stedile and B. Mançano Fernandes, *Brava Gente...*, op. cit., p. 161; Braz. Edit., p. 143.

102. Ibidem.

103. Op. cit., pp. 163-164; Braz. Edit., pp. 145-146.

104. Op. cit., p. 49; Braz. Edit., p. 43.

105. Op. cit., p. 164; Braz. Edit., p. 146.

106. J. P. Stedile, Interview by Marta Harnecker, São Paulo, May 2001.

107. Ibidem.

108. Ibidem.

109. Agricultural and cattle-raising research requires much more time than technological research in industry. Sometimes it takes 20, 30 years. Only the state can afford it.

110. J. P. Stedile, Interview by Marta Harnecker, op. cit.

111. Transgenics are organisms that have been genetically modified. Thus, transgenic products are the result of modern techniques of genetic engineering that allow some genes to be taken out of a species and transferred to another.

112. Brazilian Company for Agricultural Research.

113. J. P. Stedile, Interview by Marta Harnecker, op. cit.

114. As we have already explained, the MST had won a credit in 1986, in the middle of the democratizing process of the country; it favored those who worked in a cooperated way: the families that were members of a cooperative received double the amount than a small independent farmer, and sometimes those credits had a 50% discount.

115. In Brazilian, a dam is called a barragem.

116. United in what is known as the "Via Campesina."

117. Marcelo Enrique Batista, Interview by Natalia Alvarez, Havana, February 7, 2001.
118. A Sociedade Brasileira em Defesa do MST, in *Jornal dos Trabalhadores Rurais Sem Terra*, year XIX, N° 205, November 2000, p. 10.
119. Op. cit., p. 11.
120. César Benjamin, "*Muito Barulho por nada*," e-mail, February 6, 2001.
121. *Revista Sem Terra*, year 3, April-May-June 2000, p. 8.
122. See the development of this subject in Chapter V: The MST and its Internal Organization.

CHAPTER TWO

OCCUPY AND CAMP

As we have already seen, the Movement of Landless Workers has been developing different forms of struggle to "oppose the landowners' political and economic power" and put pressure on the government to distribute land among the farmers (1): occupations, negotiations, camping in squares and public places in the city, occupation of government buildings, public meetings, walks and marches, fasts and hunger strikes.

The Movement starts deciding the best ways to exert pressure, according to the needs of the moment and the political situation of the country. The most efficient of all has come to be occupation.

Since none of the governments have had the political will to implement agrarian reform, the occupation of the land has become a necessary weapon, and the MST's most visible action. (2)

In the 90s, about 160 000 families participated in occupations. Today there are around 500 camps with 100 000 families throughout Brazil. (3)

I – OCCUPATION

Sebastião Salgado, world-famous Brazilian photographer recognized for his images of the poorest sectors all over the planet, describes an MST occupation with the following words:

"It was impressive to see the column of landless people formed by more than 12 000 persons – in a word, 3000 families marching in the cold night of a new winter in Paraná. The army of peasants advanced in almost complete silence. You could only hear the regular panting coming from chests already used to huge efforts, and the muffled noise of feet touching the highway.

"If you watched where they were going, it was not difficult to imagine that their final destination was the Giacometi *fazenda*, one of those immense latifundia that are typical in Brazil.

"Correctly used, 83 000 hectares […] could guarantee a suitable life for the 12 000 people who marched at that time toward it.

"[…] They reached the place at dawn. […] The children and the women went toward the end of that human wave, while the men occupied their positions at the forefront of the imaginary line, ready for any encounter with the *fazenda's* 'browbeaters'.

"[…] Aware that the *fazenda's* small army does not react, the men in the vanguard break the lock and the fence begins to open; they go in; behind them, a river of peasants starts to move once again; sickles, hoes, flags are hoisted in the uncontrolled avalanche of their hopes, which have now recovered life once again, and the repressed cry of the landless people resounds as one in the light of the new day […]. (4)

TYPES OF OCCUPATION

There are different kinds of occupation according to the physical and legal characteristics of the land and the socio-political conditions of the place. (5) It is not the same to occupy land when the state or municipal governments are convinced of the need to implement agrarian reform and there is therefore a guideline not to use force against the MST, as it is when these governments represent the interests of the big landowners and are willing to use all possible methods to prevent the Movement's advance; it is not the same to implement it in places where the MST has already been working for some time, where it is admired and respected, as it is to occupy land in regions where it has been weak in its work.

The first occupations included relatively small groups of families who wanted to get a specific piece of land (6), but then – as we have already said – the need to stay within the occupation when the repressive forces came to expel them, gave them the idea to carry out massive occupations with all landless people of one territory – not to conquer that specific piece of land, but only what was necessary to settle all the families that had been mobilized in the region. As a result of this kind of occupation, usually several settlements are born. (7)

In the case of limited occupation, the size of the area they want to conquer is what determines the mobilization and organization of the families. Depending on the surface, small or numerous groups can occupy it. Each occupation of this kind represents the conquest of a settlement. Limited occupation can become massive occupation once the land is conquered and there is information about a group of areas that can be taken over by other interested families.

In some cases, when the support behind the large landowners is very strong, instead of occupying the territory, the landless people camp at the roadside to call the attention of society. This method is also used when the peasants of a region refuse to fight for land in other regions. In some places, the MST uses these camps on the roadside as a stage on which to organize that group of peasants and increase their awareness. In other cases it uses it to start grouping families until the desired number is reached.

The Movement asks its cadres to be very flexible and respect the differences in each region, taking very much into account the correlation of forces in each place in order to choose the specific form of occupation they will implement.

Some members of the MST who have participated in occupations in different places and regions of the country, now devote their time as militants to make these experiences known, organizing new occupations in order to set up new settlements.

Starting with the 90s, this work at the base has been organized by the *Frente de Massas*. This is one of the sectors of activity in which the MST is organized, but according to Christiane Campos, "it is not just one more sector or activity, it is its very heart, it pumps blood to the whole Movement. It attracts cadres for basic work, and they in turn make the MST grow on all sides." (8)

It is responsible for all activities that must be carried out during the process of occupation and conquest of the land, from the selection of the area considered convenient for occupation, to meetings with the families who will participate and the negotiations with the government.

WORK BEFORE OCCUPATION

Somehow, the moment when they go into a *fazenda* is the culmination of a path already covered by the Movement.

The first thing the MST does is to define the land to be occupied, and – if there will be a massive occupation – it must also define the nearby cities, towns and communities where there could be families interested in getting land. (9) And that is where the militants go, trying to commit them to the occupation.

Meetings at the base

This work at the base starts generally by establishing "a first contact with someone." They try for this "someone" to be "of importance within the locality: it could be the mayor, a deputy, a counsellor, it could be a union or even a priest." Someone whom the community trusts and is friendly with the Movement. (10) This person will be the "bridge" between the MST and the base; he invites the families to the first meeting, where they will speak about agrarian reform.

When there is no contact of this kind, it is the militants themselves who do this work, house by house.

At this first meeting, which can be in a schoolroom or a church, they discuss the agrarian reform in Brazil, explain what the MST is all about, why it struggles and how land can be conquered.

The question is not simply for the families to carry out the "task" of occupying land, they must understand what they are doing and why. That is why it is so important to discuss with everyone the reasons behind occupation.

Those present have questions, give their opinions and discuss. This is a very important aspect of the true participation the Movement would like. And there is no doubt that this work at the base contributes to increase the awareness of the protagonists of this struggle for land. During that first meeting they agree on the date for the next one.

For the following meeting each participant in the first one must invite other neighbors. So in general if there were ten people at the first meeting, the next one will have 20, 30, 40, and this is how they can multiply the comrades in struggle.

After four or five meetings – which are carried out in a parallel way in different communities – when there are already enough people interested in occupation, there is a regional meeting with all these families. (11) Usually they also invite a member of the MST who is already settled and he recounts his experience; they can also invite some of the better-known trustworthy leaders. At that meeting they decide the day and hour for action.

How to occupy land

The countless occupations of land the MST has successfully

organized throughout its history have given it a rich practical knowledge about how to implement them. We can summarize their teachings in the following manner:

First: the area to be occupied has to be previously identified. A study has to be made of the physical conditions of the land: existence of water, possibility for family gardens, external visibility, future productive conditions etc. It is basic to foresee possible obstacles and guarantee everything down to the smallest detail. A good selection of the land avoids having to move to another place later on, looking for better conditions while the campers await the final delivery of the land.

Second: they have to take into account that the land must be easily accessible for all families organized. Normally a latifundium is chosen in the central part of the region, close to the families who will occupy it.

Third: they must choose a piece of land that should be expropriated if the government had the political will to implement agrarian reform. (12) That is why they must try to choose an extensive area "that produces little or nothing at all – that is not fulfilling its social function." This prevents the right-wing from organizing campaigns to frighten the peasants, telling them that the MST wants to expropriate them, and it leaves the government with no arguments for the use of force to clear those lands.

This MST guideline has been modified recently because of the new decree-law passed by the Fernando Henrique Cardoso Administration, which declares that occupied lands will not be granted before two years have gone by. The Movement's answer has been to occupy productive lands as a weapon of greater pressure to obtain the unproductive lands they were aiming for in the first place. Thus, their main ally to be allotted these unproductive lands is the very owner of the latifundium in which they have settled provisionally. (14)

Fourth: it is completely necessary for the whole landless family to participate, and not just the father, as was the tradition. In this, the women's courage and initiative are usually decisive in the most critical moments of the struggle.

Fifth: they have to be as massive as possible, trying to mobilize large groups of peasants proceeding from different municipalities. (15) It is also convenient to "arrive at the place of the occupation all together to avoid the violence of the landowners." (16)

Sixth: the place and date of the occupation must be kept top secret until the very moment of the occupation. Only the leaders must know these facts (17), in order to avoid their becoming known by people who are against the Movement. We must recall that the preparatory meetings are open, so anyone who wants to participate can do so.

In this sense it is important to avoid the participation of untrustworthy people, or those who are only interested in "taking advantage of the comrades. These people give up easily, or become informants for the police and the landowners." (18)

The route to be followed must be discussed with the whole group: from the starting point to the finish line at the selected area, trying to find out if there are any detours or ways of not attracting attention, to avoid being discovered by the police or the government. (19)

Seventh: finally, they must prepare beforehand everything they will need while camping, for as long as necessary: tents, food, transportation etc. to guarantee not having to depend on outside help for a long time. (20)

LEGAL PROBLEMS

Every time there is an occupation, there are legal problems. It is important for the occupants to know that if the land belongs to the government, it is the state Federal Justice that must decide on the case, whereas if the land is private property, it is the county judge who decides. That is why if the expulsion order does not fall within one of these two categories, it is illegal. (21)

If they are expelled, they must prove the competence of the authority decreeing the expulsion and study the type of action implemented by the owner: he can come with a legal document for their expulsion (this allows them to gain time), or he can request the judge to return his lands immediately. In this case the judge can act in two different ways: decide the peasants' expulsion through police action, or convene the occupants of the land to declare before their expulsion. (22)

Based on the right given him by the Constitution, the owner can also act in "legitimate defense." (23)

NEGOTIATION

While this process of occupation goes on, the landless farmers try to negotiate with the state the settlement of these families through the Commission for Negotiations of Occupations.

Meetings (audiências)

The first step after occupation is to try to "organize meetings with the authorities, aiming at negotiating with governmental bodies." The most common result is that the workers will leave with many promises that will become empty words. "Then begins a whole process of negotiations that can go on for many years before there is a positive result." (24)

These meetings of the MST with the authorities are marked by two characteristics:

First: "the peasants always negotiate in large groups. True multitudes participate in some of the meetings, which the MST defines as massive negotiations." (25)

Second: "the peasants do not forget any of the promises they have received. They believe in what they hear. Politicians in power promise things convinced that sweet talk will quiet them down and then promises will be forgotten." (26) But this is not true, landless people do not forget and they insist again and again.

Learning througt action

Negotiation during occupation also becomes a space for learning and implies a change in the peasants' attitude before the authorities, which are now seen as their equals. "If they themselves, who had no land, were afraid to react in the past, now it is the authorities who are also afraid of their reaction, and this places them on equal terms." (27)

It is very important to look for allies among local figures and institutions: deputies, unions, and churches, to carry out negotiations in a more favorable atmosphere.

OCCUPATION AS AN INSTRUMENT FOR PRESSURE

Political pressure and negotiation

As we have already said, occupation is a form of political pressure. It aims at accelerating the negotiation. Practice has proved "that the best negotiations have come as a result of occupations" (28), because if you start by "negotiating with the government, just negotiating, you will get nothing as a result. They have no political interest in implementing agrarian reform – says a young leader of the mass movement. Then we learned: we are going to occupy the land and exert pressure; if they want to negotiate with us, fine, we either leave or give in, otherwise we stay there." (29)

Normally, if the negotiation has been well addressed and they have come to some kind of agreement in favor of future settlers, these families do not demand the same land they have occupied, but it must be land in the same region where the occupation has taken place.

What occupations aim at, then, is to "negotiate with the rulers solutions to the problems of landless peasants, and make uncultivated lands produce. That is why occupation is compared with the city workers' right to strike: it an instrument of struggle to demand their rights. Landless people have no way of striking, their possibility to exert pressure is to occupy latifundia to prove that there are uncultivated lands as well as people prepared and willing to work them and produce food." (39)

Breaking down unjust legal barriers and creating just legislation

Occupations are also a way of questioning existing legality. They show that laws have been made to benefit the dominating classes and it is up to organized movements to break down this legal barrier through pressure exerted by the people and other specific means of struggle. (31)

It is not by chance that through this means of struggle, the MST has been able to achieve legislation against the crime of dispossession in these occupations: the law would no longer penalize occupations of someone else's lands if they were idle or not adequately cultivated. This proves that only organization and pressure from the people can modify laws that benefit the richest sectors. (32)

Landless people reason in the following way: "the law protects the private property of a latifundium that concentrates the land, produces little and prevents millions of people from living in dignity." It is, therefore, "an unjust law. And no human being is forced to obey unjust laws. For many centuries, publicly and deliberately disobeying unjust laws has been an instrument of struggle of popular movements against these laws, and in favor of life." (33)

For their part, "Christians legitimize occupation of the land through the Bible, which established the Right of Redemption during sabbatical and jubilee years. This means that the person who lost the land – either he or his ancestors – had the right, every certain amount of time, to redeem it from the person who held it. It was a public law based on the principle that God gave land to everyone. If the person hoarding the land did not give it back, the person affected could use force to recover what belonged to him [...]." (34) If we accept this biblical interpretation, the peasants are occupying what belongs to them, and land accumulated in just a few hands is illegitimate.

So that occupation is legitimate, first, because it is motivated by life defense and the conquest of the means to survive; second, because it is practiced by people whom society had marginalized, and third, because it is done on unproductive lands that have no economic meaning for their owner or for society. (35)

On the other hand, many lawyers of prestige in Brazil believe that the concentration of land with no benefit for society is not only unjust, it is also illegal. "They defend the idea that occupations are not only just but legal." (36)

According to the lawyers, what a judge must do when there is an occupation is to request a technical study of the area that has been occupied, and if it is confirmed that it is a latifundium (37), they must demand its expropriation. After that they would have to assign the owners government titles (Titles of the Agrarian Reform, payable after 20 years), and demand that the workers start to produce and make the land beneficial for society.

But historically this has not been the way the judges have behaved. "They lack courage to apply the Constitution. They prefer the comfortable position of applying the Civil Code and demanding the expulsion of the families." What has been achieved is that the time-limits given by the judges for the expulsions be prolonged, thus winning more time to negotiate with the government and look for at least a provisional solution to the situation of these families. (38)

Occupations are in themselves acts of civil disobedience of existing laws, while representing at the same time "a way to put into practice the constitutional mandate to carry out agrarian reform and make all lands fulfill their social function." (39)

SUBJECTIVE VICTORIES

Expression of organized rebellion and formation of class awareness

Occupation is also a way of social questioning or organized rebellion. The action of occupying a latifundium represents an evident disobedience, which implies an enormous change in the life of landless people: it breaks down their tradition of always having to obey someone else – be it the boss, the father, the mayor – and having to bend their head (40), it breaks down two very strong feelings in the life of the peasant: fear and conformism. (41)

On the other hand, the struggle for the land is a constant struggle against capital, expropriation and exploitation. "It is an action developed by landless workers in their struggle against their exclusion by capitalists or landowners." (42) According to Salete Caldart, through occupation class struggle becomes evident: for the men and women belonging to the MST, the confrontation in which they find themselves when they occupy the large landowner's area is an experience that contributes to the peasants' class awareness: just before cutting wires and going into the area, the worker can see very clearly the contradiction and class difference – on one side, unproductive huge plots of land, a haughty bourgeoisie with the police supporting it; on the other, the workers, landless yet organized. (43)

Old values are substituted with new ones

Occupation is one of the richest experiences that prepare landless people and start "slow but deep changes" in the way they see the world.

When they occupy land, somehow the landless peasants start breaking down the supreme value of private property and telling society – and themselves – that land "must be guided by values like life and work." This is how they start destroying some values and recovering or creating others, such as that of organization. (45)

Building a new identity

For workers without even the smallest plot of land, occupying it is a way of reacting against this social condition and somehow, leaving their anonymous reality behind. When they join the Movement, they acquire a second last name: Landless. (46)

The importance of being organized

Occupation makes peasant families join others and understand personally the importance of being organized if they want the occupation to be successful and to be able to survive afterward. (47)

If instead of being collective, the occupation were individual, the peasant would be called a "criminal" or "delinquent," but since it is an organized group reaction, in general society adopts another stand. (48)

CONCLUSION

In a word, land occupation has come to be the most efficient instrument of Brazil's struggle for land. It makes peasant struggle visible and forces society to take sides. At the same time, it demonstrates that even if there are laws that help the poor, they are implemented only when there is already a social initiative. Even if Brazil's Constitution is quite progressive as far as the social function of the land is concerned, only the social pressure of the peasants has been able to accelerate the distribution of uncultivated lands to small peasants avid to work them. (49)

OCCUPATION OR INVASION?

In their effort to put public opinion against the Movement, the media define once and again the occupations carried out by the MST as "invasions," and the farmers who participate in them as "invaders"– but never as "occupants." (50)

The negative impact of the word "invasion" is evident – it is a favorite of both the government and the media (51). "To invade" is an act of force "to take something from someone." "To occupy" is to fill an empty space, in "this case, lands that do not comply with their social function." (52)

The difference stems from the fact that invasion is illegitimate, whereas occupation is legitimate. The word "invasion" would be correctly used if someone not in need of land seized a plot belonging to someone else. This term can then be applied correctly only to the multinational corporations: they have invaded millions of hectares of land throughout Brazil. (53)

II – THE CAMP

Occupation as such lasts a relatively short time: the time it takes to go into the land. Once it is occupied, the families set up camp: they prepare their provisional housing, those well-known black tents.

The camp can be set up on the land that has been occupied, on a plot handed over by the government or a private person who feels solidarity with the MST or, in the last instance, at the roadside.

The first large camp in the history of the MST is the Encruzilhada Natalino one (1981). This organizational structure consolidated itself as a result of this and other camps that followed it, becoming an important instrument to mobilize landless people in their struggle. (54)

It has three aims: to exert pressure on the authorities responsible for agrarian reform, so they will give land to the peasants who have mobilized; to educate the occupants and keep them mobilized; and to make public opinion aware of the struggle for the land. (55)

TYPES OF CAMPS

There are different types of camps, among them the provisional or the permanent ones, and within this second category, the open ones.

Provisional camps

The provisional camp is installed on a temporary basis, to attract the attention of the authorities, study and decide the path to follow and present new claims to the government. Once the time limit comes to an end or the aims are accomplished, the camp is dissolved. (56)

In 1999, for example, the MST camped for more than 100 days in front of the Curitiba Civic Center to express its repudiation for a series of expulsions and very violent attacks by the Paraná State government against peasants camped in the Querência do Norte region. During one of the expulsions, 49 peasants were unjustly detained and some were sent to prison for 70 days; others, for almost four months. "Their only crime was to fight for a piece of land," says Paulo de Marck (57), one of the landless peasants who participated in this action. The camp was installed to claim: "first, the freedom of their comrades unjustly imprisoned and the end to the persecutions by the military police, the government and state powers, of peasants from Paraná; (58) second, land for the more than 9000 families camped in the state of Paraná; and third, the assignment of the resources we the settlers need to produce." (59)

In this camp there were families from different regions of the State, 50 or 60 people from each region, all in all about 500 peasants between men, women and children. They all lived in the same barracks but organized by regions; each group had its own collective kitchen. The camp had bathrooms and showers; a place to wash clothes, with improvised tanks and piped water; a travelling school from first to fourth grades, an evening school for young people and adults; a kindergarten and a hall for political training, where people went during the daytime. They also built a bakery within the camp: part of the bread was for the campers and the other part was sold to be able to buy the necessary ingredients. There was a kitchen garden too, whose production for their own use was totally organic.

During the day, besides the activities for their training and work in the kitchen and cleaning up, commissions made up of landless peasants participated in negotiations with the government.

"If we don't light the fire under the pot, the water will never boil. The government answers workers' petitions only if there is popular pressure", says Marck.

Permanent camps

Permanent camps are thus called because they last until a solution is found for the families who have camped and they can go on for months or even years, depending on the political moment. (60)

In 1995 the MST launched in some states the experience of permanent open camps. They call them this way because the original number of families who camp grows as a result of new groups that join them. In some states the period in which they are open is limited – about 30 days, for example – and then they are closed because it is believed that a continuous increase of new groups can weaken the awareness and maturing of the group that has been camping the longest. In other states they are open as long as there are still families struggling to be settled in the region. When a group of campers is finally settled, new landless families occupy their place in the camp. In these cases the criterion followed to keep them open is that they must be massive, as a way to discourage the use of police force to expel them. (61)

Camps for the organic use of the MST

The Movement also uses camps when it must hold large meetings, such as state meetings, national congresses, massive courses etc. (62)

How to organize the camp

Camps are ideal places to start the Movement's organizational process.

You need a very good internal organization for such a large and heterogeneous number of people to carry out their lives in the camp.

Groups of families: basic organization within the MST

When landless people occupy a piece of land, they organize themselves in groups of families, in some cases even before the occupation, when preparatory meetings are held; in other cases, after the occupation itself. These groups of families are the responsibility of MST militants, who work at the base – they are mass leaders.

At the beginning the groups were small, from 8 to 10 families, but then practice proved that groups this small made up of families who knew each other before because they came from the same place provoked discussions between them for the smallest motive, thus losing their larger horizon, which was the struggle. So, even if in some camps this number is still used, in the majority of them there are from 20 to 30 families, formed by peasants from different places. This allows them to go beyond a limited vision of reality and avoids discussions on extremely domestic matters.

Since the camps usually include single people and many children, about 40 to 50 people – not a very high number – attend the meetings, but it helps create dynamic participation.

These groups of families are part of the MST structure. This is the way the Movement is organized at the base in the camps, and this should go on in the settlements. Membership is obligatory. All the families must be part of a group at the base and assume some of the different chores you must carry out within a camp.

These groups have organizational and educational aims. That is where the peasant starts to overcome his individualism and to think about more collective work; he starts working with another logic in mind.

In the end, these groups of families are the social bases for the MST.

Sectors of activities

When they start to organize camp at first with groups of families, the landless peasants also create different commissions or work teams responsible for needs related to food, health, hygiene, education, religion, animation, finances, recreation and sports etc. The participants in these bodies usually come from the people more inclined to devote their time to the Movement, who are willing to go on from obligatory work to voluntary work. Some people, for example, are responsible for tasks related to health; others, education, surveillance etc. For each one of these tasks they elect one person to be responsible for it, and he becomes part of the sector of each respective activity within the camp.

Women are outstanding in the majority of these activities, and day after day they take on more responsibilities within the Movement.

General assembly

The maximum decision-making level within the camp is the general assembly of the families who are camping. (63)

At that instance, besides analyzing and studying the steps to be taken, there are periodical studies of the situation, to examine the general atmosphere of the country as well as the general and particular conditions for struggle in that specific region and area. Some cadre from the MST gives a report on how negotiations with the state and central governments are going. This helps the campers start relating to the specific struggles within the global situation of the country.

System for general coordination

There is also a system for general coordination within the camp, whose mission is to unify work in all sectors, as well as guide the processes of negotiation and relationships with society as a whole. This coordination is made up of the leaders of the groups of families (in general, a woman and a man from each group). If the camp is very large, they elect a smaller commission so the meetings will be smoother.

Organizational principles

The principles guiding the organization within the camps are democracy, the participation of everyone in decision-making, the division of tasks and collective leadership. (64)

After some time, these principles are integrated into the daily life of the landless peasant. This implies that he must learn to build different social relations, to be a citizen who fights for the right to participate, which can start in a camp assembly and continue on to other public spaces. (65)

To be able to participate, the landless peasant must learn to listen, discuss, defend his ideas, vote on proposals, respect the opinion of his neighbor, his wife, his son, because within the camp they are all equal. (66)

Financing

In the 80s, the camps received food, clothing and medicine, mainly from communities and institutions that supported their struggle. But since the end of the 80s, their contribution has grown because of the increase in the number of settlements carried out by the MST. They cooperate in different ways: they give food, lend trucks for occupations and tractors to work the land. This support is even more significant when these settlements are associated with cooperatives.

The camp usually sustains itself with the campers' work. When the camp is on the same land they wish to conquer, they start production using mutual help.

In other situations, to help campers' families in their survival, they usually organize sources of work outside the camp. They are temporary agricultural tasks such as harvesting apples, beans, cotton etc.

The leadership of the camp organizes these tasks outside the camp, choosing a certain number of campers to carry them out on a rotating basis, because there isn't always enough work for everybody at the same time. The worker gives as much as 50% of his earnings to the camp's funds. Each week a public report is given on their earnings, so all money is used in a completely transparent way. This is done in an open assembly or in meetings of groups of families, depending on the circumstances.

In some cases, when there is a difficult economic situation, the head of the family goes to work in the city, while the rest of his family stays on in the camp. This occurs particularly in the North and Northeast regions of Brazil.

Thanks to all this support, the MST has been able to intensify the number of occupations, has increased its resistance and has been able to carry out several occupations at the same time. (67)

SPACE FOR COLLECTIVE LIFE AND SCHOOL FOR ORGANIZATION

The camp is a large space for socialization, for collective life. And at the same time, it is a school for organization.

The first concrete fact about life in the camp is that it breaks down the isolation typical of the peasant, as this space makes him live in a group; on the other hand, it is the only way to guarantee personal and family survival under those conditions. (98)

Life in camp gives each person the possibility to convert the individualism they bring with them into a more collective attitude.

Solidarity is one of the very first values that appear in the camp. To be solidary with your neighbor becomes a practical necessity: food is not enough for all, repression can be unleashed against everyone, the wind can destroy many tents, doubt and the temptation to abandon the struggle can affect each one of them or several of them at any given time.

This need for solidarity can be expressed in the following words: "victory will come for all of us or it will not come for any of us." (69) That means that this condition generates the need to learn how to be solidary and to look at reality from a collective point of view, rather than from an individual or family point of view.

They also learn to organize life in a collective way using the instances already mentioned, where each individual assumes a specific role and contributes his work to the collective task.

PERMANENCE AT THE CAMP AND VIOLENCE

To guarantee the camp's existence "is basic for the success of the struggle to conquer the land." (70)

One of the practices that characterize the MST is that the families that have been mobilized to obtain land must remain in the camp until they are assigned it. Other movements make the families return to their place of origin when negotiations begin, because they trust the promises made by the authorities. The experience of the Movement is that without the pressure of the camp, land is not given in a permanent way. (71) It has been precisely this practice of resistance that has forced judges and politicians to adopt different attitudes with respect to occupations. (72)

Expulsions and forms of resistance

Throughout the history of the MST there were "many violent and brutal expulsions, with dead people and sequels that lasted for the rest of the peasants' lives because of shootings and beatings." (73) This is the result of the unyielding positions assumed by the government or the judge, who refuse to negotiate and propose no solution.

These facts matured among the landless people their decision to resist expulsions, practice civil disobedience "as an alternative for a life in dignity." "We prefer to die fighting than to die from hunger," the peasants have expressed more than once. (74) It is a collective policy, an "instrument of struggle."

The MST favors peaceful struggle

We must explain that this decision to resist does not mean to choose violence, since the struggle favored by the MST is a peaceful one. The only weapons they use to defend themselves from police aggressions are their own bodies and work instruments: machetes, hoes, sickles, pieces of wood and old hunting rifles in desperate times. The Movement tries to avoid confronting the police, it knows it is not prepared for it, since police weapons, such as pistols, rifles, machineguns, tear gas, horses, dogs and even helicopters are much more powerful than the defensive weapons they have.

But it is not just a matter of avoiding confrontation because of these less favorable technical conditions; it avoids it mainly because their aim is not violence but the conquest of the land. As we have already observed, it is the Brazilian large landowners who want to keep their huge properties and therefore call on institutional repressive corps, or create their own (paramilitary people under contract) when those are useless.

What to do when expulsion cannot be avoided

When they cannot avoid expulsion, "the families move the camp to other areas – for example, on the roadside or on plots given them by municipalities or other institutions. When they are expelled from the roadside, they set up camp within the nearest settlements [...]." (76)

OTHER FORMS OF STRUGGLE USED BY THE CAMPERS

During the camp's existence, the Movement carries out not only an intense internal activity for organization and education, it also does external work. It unleashes a series of different activities with two aims in mind: to shake public opinion and put pressure on the authorities.

Public meetings with the authorities within the camp

The campers organize public meetings with representatives of the establishment, not in their elegant offices but in the place occupied by them, "to make them feel close up the situation suffered by the campers and for them to express their intentions directly to the mass of people gathered there." (77)

Walks or marches

They also promote walks or marches. The idea of the marches came up as an answer to a tactics promoted by the government to isolate the MST from society. The media did not publish anything on occupations taking place and systematically ignored their partial struggles. While searching for what to do under these circumstances, the MST came to the conclusion that if it organized walks that would go through different towns it would be a good formula to face the negative campaign the government and the right were carrying out. (78) Marches kill several birds with one stone: they call the attention of the media and the population on the land problem and the objectives the MST struggles to attain, and they put pressure on the politicians.

Some marches have covered more than 500 kilometers of road, crossing through towns and cities. They sleep anywhere, they organize public meetings and participate in gatherings and celebrations throughout their journey, "making the population aware of the need for agrarian reform and involving them in the struggle." The MST has been able to convoke more than a million people in these activities. (78)

Taking advantage of Brazil's agricultural cycle and to commemorate the international journey in favor of the peasant struggle, practically every year in April the MST – sometimes by itself, at other times with other movements – also organizes local activities in state capitals.

"Depending on the situation of rural workers, the political atmosphere and the attitudes of the rulers, these walks can become a detonator of social conflict." (80)

Public fast and hunger strikes

Public fast and hunger strikes have not been much used by the MST. Public fast consists in not eating voluntarily in a public place. This action aims at showing how hungry peasants go day after day and "the peaceful attitude of landless peasants, their readiness to talk, proving to public opinion that those who accuse them of being guerrilla fighters lie." (81)

In general, they fast for a specific amount of time (three to five days), until the rulers decide to listen to the workers' claims.

Hunger strikes are an instrument of struggle used only in extreme situations, "with a lot of opinions and preparation, tied to a permanent process of pressure on the authorities, making public opinion demand from the government that it avoid putting the strikers' life in danger." It is justified only "when an increasing number of lives are in danger and nothing is done to save them." (82)

Occupation of public buildings

As a result of the indifference some governments or institutions related to agrarian reform show for the landless peasants' claims, the MST has been forced to look for stronger methods to exert pressure: the occupation of public buildings linked to concrete claims. These occupations aim at revealing that those responsible for the negotiation have not fulfilled their promises.

"We occupy Incra, for example – it is in charge of guaranteeing subsidies for agriculture – to demand that the government settle the families and give them subsidies for agrarian reform. Until we get an answer we do not leave," declares Marcelo Enrique Batista, who has participated in some of these actions. (83)

Usually the MST uses this form of struggle when the representatives of the government give no answer or refuse to receive them.

Some of these occupations can last several days and they are a way to exert permanent pressure. (84)

Camps in public places

When the situation requires it, the landless peasants set up camps in the center of cities, trying to put pressure on the authorities until they decide to answer their claims.

There is no doubt that a camp outside the countryside produces a strong impact – at least from a visual point of view – among city people, used to close their eyes in front of other people's problems.

Almost always, the rulers have this kind of action eliminated. (85) They do not like to have under their own nose evident proof of their malpractice.

Reoccupation

The campers can reoccupy a latifundium from which they have been expelled. This depends on the general situation, the atmosphere, negotiations with the government and the living conditions of those camping. A new occupation becomes a way to demand agility and political commitment from the government. (86)

NOTES

1. João Pedro Stedile and Frei Sérgio, *La lucha por la tierra en el Brasil,* MST, São Paulo, 1999, p. 28.
2. Some say that the MST "was born with land occupations, their stron-

gest characteristic, which materializes, perhaps like no other action, the option of struggle for land." Roseli Salete Caldart, *Pedagogia do Movimento Sem Terra*, Editora Vozes, 2000, p. 108.

3. These numbers come from preliminary MST studies. "The majority of the camps are organized by the MST. But there are several others linked to the union movement, the CPT and other regional bodies and organizations struggling for land." *(Jornal dos Trabalhadores Rurais Sem Terra*, year XIX, N° 206, December 2000/January 2001, pp. 8-9).
4. This text by Salgado belongs to his paper *Terra* 1996.
5. Ivanette Tonin, interview by Marta Harnecker, Havana, November 16, 2001. The following information comes from her testimony.
6. B. Mançano Fernandes, *A Formação do MST no Brasil*, Editora Vozes, Petrópolis, p. 291.
7. Ibidem.
8. Christiane Campos, interview by Marta Harnecker, Montreal, February 20, 2001.
9. Work at the base can include one or several municipalities in the same micro-region, several municipalities in several micro-regions, or even more than one state in the frontier areas. B. Mançano Fernandes, *A Formação do...*, op. cit., p. 284.
10. Marcelo Enrique Batista, member of the MST Front of the Masses and student at the Latin-American School for Medical Sciences, interview by Natalia Alvarez, Havana, February 7, 2001.
11. Meetings at the base can last "one, three, six months or even years, depending on the situation." (B. Mançano Fernandes, *A Formação do...*, op. cit., p. 284).
12. J. P. Stedile and Frei Sérgio, *La lucha por la tierra ...*, op. cit., p. 30.
13. Never smaller than 700 hectares, and in some regions like Mato Grosso, no fewer than 1500 hectares.
14. Ivanette Tonin, interview by Marta Harnecker, op cit.
15. J. P. Stedile and Frei Sérgio, *La lucha por la tierra...*, op. cit. p. 29.
16. MST, *Construindo o Caminho*, São Paulo, June 1986, p. 73.
17. Ibidem.
18. Ibidem.
19. Ibidem.
20. Ibidem.

21. Op. cit., p. 78.
22. Op. cit., pp. 78-79.
23. Op. cit., p. 79.
24. J. P. Stedile and Frei Sérgio, *La lucha por la tierra...*, op. cit., p. 28.
25. Ibidem.
26. Op cit., pp. 28-29.
27. R. Salete Caldart, *Pedagogia do Movimento...*, op. cit., p. 122.
28. J. P. Stedile and Frei Sérgio, *La lucha por la tierra...*, op. cit., p. 30.
29. Marcelo Enrique Batista, interview by Natalia Alvarez, op. cit.
30. J. P. Stedile and Frei Sérgio, *La lucha por la tierra...*, op. cit., p. 33.
31. Jose Maschio, electronic mail, October 25, 2000 (document).
32. Ibidem.
33. J. P. Stedile and Frei Sérgio, *La lucha por la tierra...*, op. cit., pp. 30-31.
34. Op. cit., p. 34.
35. Op. cit., p. 33.
36. Op. cit., p. 31.
37. From ancient Rome the term *latifundium* is used to describe the control by one single owner over a large piece of land. But the significance of "great extension" varies according to the realities of each country, and to the local realities within the same country. For example, in Japan, with a very populated small surface, a property of land is considered a latifundium if it is larger than 100 hectares. But Brazil has an enormous yet unpopulated surface. Here we consider the presence of a latifundium when it covers more than 1000 hectares. But in Brazil itself, "due to the different characteristics of each region, the concept of latifundium has different dimensions according to the region. In Rio Grande do Sul, for example, an area with more than 500 hectares could be considered a latifundium. But in the Amazonic States, a property covering 1000 hectares would not." In general, latifundia are areas with over 5000 hectares, and in Brazil there are owners who have more than a million hectares. (J. P. Stedile, "*Latifúndio: O Pecado Agrário Brasileiro*", 1999, document).
38. J. P. Stedile and Frei Sérgio, *La lucha por la tierra,* op. cit., p. 31.
39. Op. cit., pp. 30-31.
40. R. Salete Caldart, *Pedagogia do Movimento...*, op. cit., p. 110.

41. "When they occupy the land they learn to disobey, thus rebelling against a fate of death." (Ibidem.)
42. B. Mançano Fernandes, *A Formação do...*, op. cit., p. 280.
43. R. Salete Caldart, *Pedagogia do Movimento...*, op. cit., p. 111.
44. Op. cit., p. 108.
45. Op. cit., p. 111.
46. Op. cit., p. 109.
47. Marta Harnecker, *Construyendo una fuerza social antineoliberal*, article in Vozes, Petrópolis, 2000, p. 52.
48. R. Salete Caldart, *Pedagogia do Movimento...*, op. cit., p. 109.
49. M. Harnecker, *Construyendo...*, op. cit., p. 52.
50. J. P. Stedile and Frei Sérgio, *La lucha por la tierra...*, op. cit., pp. 32-33.
51. Ibidem.
52. Gomes da Silva in R. Salete Caldart, *Pedagogia do Movimento...*, op. cit., p. 109.
53. J. P. Stedile and Frei Sérgio, *La lucha por la tierra...*, op. cit., p. 33.
54. R. Salete Caldart, *Pedagogia do Movimento...*, op. cit., p. 114.
55. Ibidem.
56. J. P. Stedile and Frei Sérgio, *La lucha por la tierra...*, op. cit., p. 35.
57. Paulo de Marck, interview by Marta Harnecker, Curitiba, September 1999.
58. "During Jaime Lerner's present government – says Paulo de Marck – there were more than 15 comrades dead and more than 250 detained, many tortured, others beaten by the police."
59. Paulo de Marck, interview by Marta Harnecker, op. cit.
60. R. Salete Caldart, *Pedagogia do Movimento...*, op. cit., p. 114. This kind of camp is also called a "structural camp" because it is part of the very structure of the MST (Christiane Campos, interview by Marta Harnecker, op. cit.).
61. Ivanette Tonin, interview by Marta Harnecker, op. cit.
62. Op. cit.
63. R. Salete Caldart, *Pedagogia do Movimento...*, op. cit., p. 115.
64. J. P. Stedile and Frei Sérgio, *La lucha por la tierra...*, op. cit., p. 39.
65. R. Salete Caldart, *Pedagogia do Movimento...*, op. cit., p. 117.
66. Op. cit., p. 118.

67. B. Mançano Fernandes, *A Formação do...*, op. cit., p. 294.
68. R. Salete Caldart, *Pedagogia do Movimento...*, op. cit., p. 116.
69. Ibidem.
70. B. Mançano Fernandes, *A Formação do...*, op. cit., p. 296.
71. Ibidem.
72. J. P. Stedile and Frei Sérgio, *La lucha por la tierra...*, op. cit., p. 32.
73. Op. cit., p. 31.
74. Op. cit., pp. 31-32.
75. Op. cit., p. 32.
76. B. Mançano Fernandes, *A Formação do...*, op. cit., p. 296.
77. J. P. Stedile and Frei Sérgio, *La lucha por la tierra,* op. cit., p. 35.
78. Ivanette Tonin, interview by Marta Harnecker, op. cit.
79. J. P. Stedile, notes to this work, November 4, 2001.
80. J. P. Stedile and Frei Sérgio, *La lucha por la tierra...*, op. cit., pp. 35-36.
81. Op. cit., p. 36.
82. Ibidem.
83. Interview by Natalia Alvarez, op. cit.
84. J. P. Stedile and Frei Sérgio, *La lucha por la tierra...*, op. cit. p. 37.
85. Ibidem.
86. Op. cit., p. 38.

CHAPTER THREE

THE SETTLEMENTS

I – Settlements within the mst

Once the land conquered and its property made legal, as a result of a generally quite long struggle, the peasants settle on the lands assigned them. These agricultural communities are called "settlements." (1)

It is important to explain that the word settlement has been adopted only recently in Brazil. It appears in the mid 60s. For "social movements struggling for land, a settlement is synonymous with conquered land. For the state it is an area destined to a group of landless families and a way to solve the problem of the land." (2)

Settlements are very different. There are places where 20 to 30 families install themselves, while in others there are 600 or 700, though this is not the most frequent situation. On the other hand, regional characteristics, the distance from the markets and the quality of the land they have received determine important differences between them.

One of the characteristics of MST settlements is "their concern for the organization of production and, together with it, the definition of a more general strategy for organizing life in the settlement as a whole, related to the wider struggle for strategy defined by the Movement." (3)

There are general guidelines for the process of organizing the settlements, but the MST takes special care to point out that they must be applied in a differentiated way. Each settlement must design its own path, interpreting the Movement's guidelines according to its own situation. It must make decisions according to its specific circumstances, the kind of organization it has adopted and the way in which it leads the new life for the peasants on conquered land. "That is why there are no two similar settlements, but there are characteristics that identify them as fractions of a territory occupied by the MST." (4)

The settlements increasingly become the economic and political rearguard of the struggle for agrarian reform in Brazil. They contribute most of the financing and free cadres so they can devote their time to organizing the Movement in other regions of the country.

It is important to explain that not all peasants in a camp receive their land simultaneously. (5)

At the beginning, Incra (6) made a census of the families, which were also interviewed on an individual basis, and with these data it prepared a list of points according to which it distributed the land. This is how the first settlements were constituted; for example the Anoni *Fazenda* one, in Rio Grande do Sul. Then the MST got the official institution to respect – when assigning land – the groups of families that had already been formed in the camps because of the affinities of its members. The Movement handed Incra the list of families that made up the group and the area they were interested in, and the institution accepted these criteria. It was the first victory. Another came later: the MST succeeded in having land assigned through raffles so*land distribution would be a transparent process; the raffles were done by groups of families.

In other places, where there are "permanent camps", they combine the raffle with the seniority of the peasants.

The lands where the peasants settle can come from expropriated private latifundia or from state lands. In the first case, the government compensates the owners of the land for their investments: fences, houses, warehouses etc., and gives them titles for the expropriated land, called Titles of Agrarian Debt (TDAs), paid in twenty years or more. (8) In some cases, to accelerate the proceedings – since the expropriation process is very slow – the government decides to purchase the lands from the landowners instead of expropriating them, paying with titles of agrarian debt but in ten years' time. Recently, the government has benefited expropriated landowners by allowing them to use their titles to purchase stock in state companies that have been made private. In the case of public lands, they are given over by the government to be worked by landless farmers.

We shall now analyze two concrete experiences on the organization of some settlements, one in Pirituba, State of São Paulo, and the other one in Santa Catarina, on the frontier with Argentina. We think it is important for the reader to follow step by step what happened in these cases, as has been explained by the leaders of the MST who live in these settlements, before going on to study the basic lessons the Movement has learned from them and from other experiences throughout the whole country.

II – SETTLEMENTS IN THE *FAZENDA* PIRITUBA

The following text is the testimony given by Delwek Mateus, leader of the MST in the State of São Páulo, in an interview by Marta Harnecker in May 2001. Mateus has always devoted his time within the Movement to the task of working with the settlements and the organization of cooperatives in that state. He was a member of church communities at the base before participating in the *Fazenda*'s Pirituba occupation and joining the MST.

OCCUPATION

At the beginning of the 80s, through the mediation of rural workers' unions and the support of the Catholic Church, knowing the law protected them (9), landless people from the São Paulo region started to organize themselves to claim from the government uncultivated lands of the *Fazenda* Pirituba. (10)

They held meetings with the government; with the secretaries directly responsible for these areas; with mayors, counsellors – in a word, with several authorities of the State of São Paulo. But this was not enough to recover the land, and get them to comply with the law. That is when they decided to occupy the *fazenda*.

REPRESSION OF SMALL GROUPS

From 1980 to 1984, a small group of landless peasants – between 30 and 50 families – carried out different occupations in these areas. The large landowners immediately sent their salaried gangsters (11) to expel the families.

Those years were marked by repeated conflicts between landless peasants and large landowners. There were many expulsions. The workers then understood the need to enlarge the group and improve their organization.

Massive occupation: 300 Families break the fence

Preparatory meetings were held in the parishes and the rural workers' union headquarters of the region. The group started growing as a result of the discussions with landless workers.

On May 13, 1984, with about 300 landless families – around 1000 people, including men, women and children – we broke down the fence at the *Fazenda* Pirituba.

The families – mostly peasant families – came from different municipalities of the region, including from the state of Paraná. (12) That was my case. I came with my family and 30 more people.

We camped on the land we wanted and finally won. It was one of Brazil's first camps of landless peasants, when the MST didn't exist yet in São Paulo.

Organize to resist in the camp

Starting with the occupation, the whole process of confrontation with the landowner, demanding the state etc. repeated itself, but as we were a large group, we were able to resist the landowners' reaction and this time their gangsters were unable to expel us.

Our main worry was how to organize ourselves and survive. Thanks to the CPT (13) that supported us, we tried to get information on the experiences developed in Rio Grande do Sul. From them we learned the need to organize the camp in groups of families and work: security, food, negotiation, health, education etc. Our process to organize ourselves was similar to the experiences in the South.

We started out with groups of 10 to 15 families, which were close to each other because of their affinities. For example, those who came from the same neighborhood and had been living together for a long time. From these groups we organized work teams inside the camp.

Selection of the families to be settled

During the struggle – it lasted about four months – there were families who gave up and others who did not have the conditions to be accepted.

The criteria for selection were analysed among all of us. We decided on the following: be a landless rural worker, have no income at all, not to be a public officer, have children so the land could be cultivated by the family itself, have previous experience, and have been in the region for some time.

The peasants who were camped and the state participated in

the definition of the number of families to be settled and the size of the area corresponding to each. We took into account the specific agriculture of the region before defining the size of the land to be assigned each family so it could have enough income to live in minimum conditions.

These definitions allowed us to choose 150 families. We could have had more if it had been necessary, 170 or 180, because we could have reduced a little the size of the plot handed to each family.

Since we were able to get two plots of land to settle the families, we had to separate in two groups: one made up of 95 families and the other 55. Since the land was quite uniform there were no problems.

Even though our land has been well defined between the two groups, sometimes both lands are used in a collective way, or sometimes we have come together to use the same machines or instruments.

Since the *Fazenda* Pirituba was very large and we occupy only a small part of it, other families from the region – interested in our experience – organized themselves and promoted new occupations. So in 1986 a third group was created; a fourth in 1988; the fifth in 1990; and the sixth in 1992. These groups came up during a ten-year period and implied 360 families. Today there are six groups: the biggest is the first one, with about 100 families, while the others average 50. All of them have carried out more or less similar experiences. At the beginning they were a collective association; later they formed smaller groups. Today there are several cooperatives as well as different informal groups, and they are all part of the Regional Cooperative.

ORGANIZATION OF THE SETTLEMENT

Initially, cooperated production

Since the majority of the families that were camped were peasants from the region, in our case what happened was that before getting the authorization for the use of land, we had already analysed how we would use it and we already knew what we would sow. When the government sent a group of technicians to advise the settlement, we were already organized and were able to discuss our proposal for collective work.

Both groups were organized in two *agrovilas*. (14) The idea came up immediately to use collective work to start clearing the underbrush, because the land had been abandoned and it was in a terrible condition.

Later on, since we knew that the quality of the land was bad and we needed capital to work it, we created two associations to put pressure on the state for the credit necessary to purchase tractors. It was our first collective action.

With those tractors we worked 50% of the land we had been assigned. The first corn, beans and rice harvests were good and we used them to feed the families during the first year.

This kind of organization guaranteed a good production. It was very important for two reasons: first, to guarantee food for the families; second: to prove society of the region that we were not a bunch of tramps, but that we wanted to work, to produce, and that agrarian reform was possible, because society had reacted questioning occupation and agrarian reform.

Birth of family groups

This experience with collective work and association lasted during the first two or three years. Each group had its own experience. But from 1987-1988 we started to understand that this method did not please everybody, there were those who wanted to produce in a different way. That is how another discussion took place in this context: how to organize ourselves. Then the idea came up to create groups of families. Until then there was only one single large group, but from that moment on we had the idea to organize smaller groups, and that is the system we still have today.

At present, each settlement is organized in groups of 8 to 30 families. Some have chosen to form cooperatives, others constitute informal groups. There are experiences of more or less collective work.

These groups of families have experienced three ways to produce: completely collective work (such as the Agricultural and Cattle-Raising Cooperatives, CPAs); combined work, where collective production goes hand in hand with individual production; and individual work, even though in some cases there is some kind of cooperation, with the use of machinery, for example.

Difficulties managing large units

Several things determined some peasants to abandon collective work after a few years. One of them was the difficulty to manage efficiently the Association of the Pirituba Settlement, for it became a large concern that managed an extensive farming area, several machines and an important volume of resources. It was difficult to manage all that and understand how it should work. There was a lot of criticism because the people were unable to control this huge financial and administrative body.

Smaller groups facilitate participation

In smaller groups everything is easier. Their volume of work – even financial and administrative work – is much less and that helps understanding and participation. The person who does not understand, questions, and does not feel stimulated to participate.

In larger formal meetings, things are more difficult, because there is a kind of argument, one group goes against the other, an idea is put against the other; participation is usually very limited, since the people wishing to express their suggestions or their ideas, do not dare to do so. But in everyday life they do.

After my own experience, I believe that before creating a large association there must be a process to train the peasants, for a broader understanding and vision of the political, cultural, ideological and economic world – in a word, they must increase their awareness. While they acquire this capacity they will be able to understand a more complex administration and go on to regional structures for participation.

Thus you build a whole process from the smaller groups, with an integral participation of the families, go on to a second stage with the participation of representatives from those groups, until you have a broader regional structure, headed by representatives from the groups at the base. This is what we are trying to do: to create a broader experience involving other aspects of life in the settlements through representatives of the groups of families.

Agrovilas and ways to distribute lots

We discussed how to place the houses. The peasants quite strongly rejected living in an *agrovila*, while understanding its advantages.

To solve this situation we tried to respect the peasants' desire to have at least some kind of products growing around their home. We now have smaller lots where we build the houses, and they plant yucca, potatoes, vegetables, raise some animals that will not eat the neighbor's vegetables. Besides these lots we have larger lots farther away, where the cooperatives work on their products.

There is also a community center shared by all settlements, where you can find the school, the health center, the church, the sports and recreational areas, and the community radio.

This flexibility and the respect for the peasant's desire to have his own lot near his house have been very important to make the families feel well. There are no families wishing to leave the settlement, they are all satisfied.

Life in *agrovilas* helps social relations. If each family had lived on its own individual lot, kilometers away from each other, it would have been much more difficult to exchange ideas and analyze problems. But since they live close to one another, there are more contacts and this helps, because people meet, chat, talk about their problems and what they are thinking. It is this social interrelation that contributes to the organization and the solution of problems.

And why not a collective dining room

Though we know that in some settlements the collective dining room has become an excellent place for these interrelations, we believe that in our case it would not work. The Pirituba settlement reflects – though on a smaller scale – the cosmopolitan characteristic of São Paulo, whose population is made up of migrant people from Rio Grande do Sul, Paraná, Pernambuco, Bahia, Minas Gerais and, in a smaller number, from São Paulo itself. Eating habits are very different. For example, there are people from Minas Gerais who like cheese, and there are those from Bahia who like other things.

Property titles to the land

We don't yet have a property title for our land because the state is very slow, bureaucratic and so far has not given us an official document. But that does not worry us. What really guarantees staying on the land is precisely our organization and the use of the land. The law decides that the state must give a concession for the use of the land, and not a final property title.

If a family decides to leave, it cannot sell the land, but it has the right to be paid for whatever it has built on it: the house, investments on the soil, the fence etc. Then that land is assigned to another landless family of the region waiting for this opportunity. There is a list made by both the MST and Incra. The Movement proposes families who have been camped, and in general, the government wants the mayors – or other people with political influence – to name them.

After that, the selected families that fulfill the requirements participate in a raffle to be assigned their lot of land.

COOPERATIVES

Pirituba is the only settlement in the region, but we are in contact with small traditional farmers and we work with them to get them to join the MST, both in production and in political and ideological work, so they will participate with us in the struggle.

The regional cooperative

As I was telling you, here in Pirituba we have several kinds of cooperation: Cooperatives for Agricultural and Cattle-Raising Production that work in a collective way; mixed cooperatives, that combine collective and individual production; and informal groups that go into some kind of cooperation.

These different cooperatives and informal groups belong to an MST regional cooperative. At this higher instance they analyze the broader aspects of the organization at a regional level and try to become a place in which the workers can participate.

Their economic aim is to support marketing and improve products through the small agricultural and cattle-raising industries.

The regional cooperative's task is mainly an economic one. They need, therefore, a broader structure to attend to the other aspects of the life of the settled peasants, such as the cultural, social, health and educational aspects.

Cooperative labor force

In production cooperatives, work is carried out by the associated peasants, in particular the young ones. This is a way to open up new sources of work for the youth.

As far as the distribution of surplus products is concerned, initially we distributed them equally among all the families, without taking into account how much each had contributed in work hours. This method caused us many problems: it ended by not stimulating the people who made the greatest efforts because it did not reward the different amount of work of each partner, but rather it encouraged loafing around, precisely at a time in which we most needed to increase production. Then we went on to the formula to distribute these products according to the days worked and, finally, according to the hours worked. We have set up a system to control this and at the end of the year we distribute surplus production according to the hours worked. This formula is better than the previous ones because it stimulates the person who works more, but it is still not perfect because each partner's productivity is not the same: a young and strong partner can harvest much more corn in one hour that an older and weaker partner can. The young people are not satisfied because they produce more than their elders but receive the same quantity. We haven't yet found the most effective formula to measure the work of each member of the cooperative. This is much more difficult in agricultural and cattle-raising tasks than in industrial ones.

Besides this payment according to the hours worked, the Movement believes that it must carry out at the same time a mystique for work, and find different ways to emulate.

Problems in cooperatives

Machinery and labor force
Talking about machinery, I have to recognize that we made the error of purchasing them without a previous plan of what to do with the labor force that would be substituted by the machine.

In our settlement we have a huge infrastructure: we have made very high investments in tractors, harvesters and trucks, because seeds are our main production: corn, beans and wheat, that depend greatly on machines and little on labor force.

Strong dependence on modern technology
We have a very concrete problem – it is not a little problem but

a big one: our machines, our instruments, our techniques for production depend largely on the conventional technological package made up of specific machines, hybrid seeds, agricultural fertilizers and herbicides – the so-called modern technology. We have to free ourselves from this dependence, but first we must go through a transitional period, since our production cooperatives were organized on this model. Today we are debating these aspects both in the settlement and in the national MST.

Credits linked to a technological package

This is not an easy task because we are assigned credits and technical assistance around this package. We have to purchase machines, huge tractors and instruments often inappropriate for the size of the land, and on top, they liberate a lot of labor force.

On the other hand, it is a very expensive technological package that depends greatly on multinational corporations. Besides eating up all the worker's income, these products harm the environment and our health.

Our production is excellent, abundant, one of the best in the state as far as quantity is concerned, but it generates no income because it is based on an expensive model.

The logic of the market versus the logic of solidarity

In our cooperatives we have not met the aims we had set ourselves for cheaper marketing and competitiveness. That is where our limit is, the system does not allow it.

Today, the cooperatives devote themselves to concrete small initiatives to improve the income and the production of the settlers. They can be very varied: from small agro-industries to marketing directly to the consumer through a regional popular market, to mention only a few.

One of the most difficult things to do is to be efficient and competitive within the existing capitalist model, while trying to be economically positive. That is why what we need are practical alternatives to improve both the settlers' income and the conditions to support price fluctuations, by diversifying production, stimulating alternative production, lowering costs, creating a local market for the products of these agro-industries.

These initiatives can be promoted by regional cooperatives, but they must understand clearly the change they mean. The thing is not to compete within the existing model, but to find concrete alternatives. Today, this is the responsibility of the MST cooperatives.

Bourgeois legality

On the other hand, legality imposed by capitalism also imposes limitations: they cut off our credits, technical assistance, they harass us with audits, accusations, and impede marketing. It is evident that they put limitations on us because today, the MST is the main enemy of the government, of the bourgeois project; because we question their model, mainly the agricultural one.

If the government and the bourgeoisie can block us through cooperatives it is because these are forced to work within legislation in force. They fix the rules of the game. We can go forward as long as they want us to, but when they no longer want that, they put limitations on us.

Low participation from women and young people

Another problem stemming from the practice of the organization itself is the low participation of women and young people, both in the cooperatives and in the community.

Usually, cooperatives are headed by men, though legislation admits the participation of women. The MST is working to guarantee the participation of both groups, not only in the cooperatives but also in the active life of the families working individually. They want to have women participating in the decisions related to what and how they are going to produce. We have the experiences of the CPAs, where the participation of women is on a par to that of the men. She is one more partner in the cooperative, with the same rights and duties. It is an interesting process, at least in some of our cooperatives this experience already exists.

An alternative organic agriculture

We will have to rebuild these cooperatives reorganizing the instruments and production techniques (machinery, tools, use of the soil). We will have to produce our own seeds and avoid the use of chemical fertilizers and chemicals.

There are already some small alternative experiences to build this new proposal. But undoubtedly this process will require several years, because the implementation of something different, like organic agriculture, will have to go through a costly process of adaptation. The problem is: who pays for this while the transition is going on? We believe it should be society, through state subsidies, or direct marketing through an organized community prepared to fight for this. The small farmer cannot pay for this, he has no accumulation of capital and during the transition period he will have no income whatsoever. One thing prevents the other. He does not do it because he cannot go hungry. That is the limitation for the process of change.

We hope to carry it through, but there are very few experiences because we have no resources to assume the cost.

Honey as an alternative production

An example of a concrete alternative to the existing model is the production of honey, just now beginning at the Itapeva settlement with the support of the regional MST cooperative.

We are building a small factory that will benefit the honey produced in the region, including that of small farmers, and this will also stimulate production.

This initiative is aimed at increasing the income of the settlers, without having to depend on the state or on multinational corporations, nor having to compete with them. This advantage is multiplied by the fact that honey is a healthy food for the families and it requires neither toxics for agriculture nor credits, because the bees work by themselves.

Another alternative we have started is a nursery to stimulate planting timber – and fruit-yielding trees.

This is a long-range task and it will require much persistence and patience, since everything we now have follows the existing model, and it is not easy to build something different.

We don't yet have any agro-industry in our settlement, but we do have small initiatives, very rustic ones at that, like a small production of pork meat.

We have also started on the production of home-made sweets. This activity is in the hands of women from one of the areas of the settlement. It is a very rich experience because many women participate in it.

One of the reasons why agro-industry did not go forward in our settlement was the kind of production we had: corn and beans. The installation of an agro-industry for this kind of production would demand a big investment. Since they do not have sufficient capital, the settlers are forced to sell their production to buyers from the region. Big agro-industries in the South or even here in the State of São Paulo, in Pontal do Paranapanema, were built with resources from Procera. Since many families made up the cooperative, the total sum of each individual credit came to enough money to invest in large agro-industries. But here, since we had a small number of settlers, the volume of the Procera credit was not enough to install a large factory, as we would have liked to.

I still consider that it is a positive thing not to have been able to do it because I believe it allows us to work on the idea of transition toward an alternative production to the existing technological model.

If we had installed an agro-industry, it would be more difficult because we would have to make it work, and for that we depend on the existing model.

The present situation allows us to think about small agro-industries. Our great project is to install small agro-industries, including some rustic ones, to stimulate the participation of the comrades, the women and the young people, both in the work itself and in the management of the project. We want to convert these small agro-industries in a potential for production here in the region, and even use them as a stepping-stone to find a way to market the product locally.

The first thing we must do is to increase the awareness of the peasants, so they can understand the proposal. They will accept it only if they understand it. This will require plenty of work to train them on the long term in theory and practice: the peasants like to see concrete applications; this makes things understandable for them.

Increase the range of cooperation to include the social and cultural spheres

We have to go forward to a broader cooperation, because it does not stop at the economic aspect of the cooperatives. This cooperation must push the social and cultural organization of the settlements forward: it must increase the workers' political and ideological awareness. If we do not go forward, it will be very difficult to overcome the resistance we have to oppose now, a sort of "special period" (17), that we are going through, and that requires an organized base for the MST.

Our base must be organized in all directions: in economic production and in social and cultural awareness. We must also recover our peasant culture, because now we depend a lot on the culture imposed by capitalism. That is the great jump forward in quality that we must take today!

But to achieve this we must go a step beyond cooperatives.

Since their main aim is their economic result and the fight for the market, everything organized around the cooperative is very concentrated on productive results, in improving agro-industry and marketing, and that what the settlers produce be income-yielding, so they can increase their incomes.

At the beginning we were very happy with the economic efficiency of the cooperatives and we did not worry about the social and cultural aspects or the political and ideological ones, we believed the economic possibility of the cooperatives would suffice to guarantee the organization of our base. But it didn't turn out that way, because not even the cooperatives became income-yielding organizations.

We are criticizing ourselves and we are aware of the resistance we have before us and of the need to prepare a new proposal for the settlements' organization, based on a broader cooperation.

To guarantee our resistance we need a broad organizational process. We must organize the communities, even if they are not formally incorporated into the cooperatives, because the majority of our settlers are not.

The MST must approach those settlers and have them become part of the organized base of the Movement; we must work on the educational, health, recreational and cultural aspects. This is also cooperation, and therefore the Cooperative System should participate in it.

EDUCATION

The settlement has some very good experiences in the productive sphere. But we are also present in other spheres, such as education and health. And now we are beginning to work on culture and recreation.

The school system

In the case of Pirituba, education of the landless peasants follows the policy of the state.

Primary education is given in the settlement's own school, though it belongs to the public network and the teachers are under state contract. But secondary schooling must be done in the cities.

The government of São Paulo adopted the policy of eliminating the numerous junior high schools existing in rural communities, with the argument that education in the countryside was very expensive and there was a great advantage for peasant children to study in the city, where education was better. To take the children to these schools we have transportation paid for by the state. We won that battle.

But we are against this policy. We start from a theoretical and practical proposal: if the people are farmers and live in the country, it is there that they must develop their practical knowledge from childhood. Education for the children of the farmers must be in the countryside, where they can see how plants are born and grow, the animals, production, how their parents work. This is basic in people's cultural education. If we want peasants to exist in the future, we must start building them from childhood.

Education within the settlement is much better than that of peasants in general. Since they are better organized, the settlers have more power to put their claims before the state. Through the MST educational sector, we also contribute to improve the quality of teaching within the settlement.

Only a few teachers are militants

In Pirituba there are few teachers who are also militants of the MST because of the requirements to get a contract in the public network: they must have finished their secondary schooling and participate in a public competition. But this does not mean our teachers do not participate, suggest, guide, talk, and discuss our own proposal.

Our role is to control and put pressure on the state so it will improve conditions in education. And through our militants we must also improve the very quality of teaching, talking with the teachers and analysing ideas with them, explaining the MST's proposal for education. This process has been going on from the beginning of the settlement. It is not ideal yet, but we have good experiences thanks to effective participation.

This situation has forced us to teach the children the history and principles of the Movement outside school, but this is not easy to do. We try to slowly convince the teachers so they will start introducing these subjects. Meanwhile we must work directly with the landless children, to start forming them ideologically. That is why the teaching group must find different ways to do it: activities with the children, analysis with the teachers and parents etc.

HEALTH

In Pirituba we have a good experience in this, and we try to have the state participate and contribute to our proposal. But there are many diverse opinions, so this also is a building process.

Join the MST proposal with traditional midicine
The MST's health proposal is based on health prevention and medicinal plants.

We are still in the process of formulating our proposal nationally. So far we have developed local experiences, even if they involve other regional and state groups.

We are trying to combine this with the federal government's program, called "family doctor," which has signed agreements with state governments. In some states this is making progress while in others it is not. This program has nothing to do with Cuba's. It is a very precarious family doctor.

Here we have a doctor and some sanitary workers paid for by the state, and periodically they come to visit our health center in the settlement to take care of the families.

To improve this work we are trying to join our work in preventive health to that of the doctor and the workers. Some of our militants are discussing with this group and proposing the unification of our efforts in order to improve health in general.

Not all settlements have health centers

Not all settlements have health centers, but at least two of them will. And the doctor comes to three places in the settlements, two days each. He takes care of neighboring families. There is another health center close to a neighborhood of small farmers of the region, where the doctor sees our settlers as well as the small farmers.

The interesting part is that our proposal is being discussed with the small farmers too.

Alternative medicine

Within the settlement we have a drugstore for alternative medicine and a medicinal garden, and some of our militants know how to prepare medicine.

The doctor likes our health proposal, and this is important. We are talking with him so he can prescribe the medicine we make in the settlement.

III – "CONQUISTA DA FRONTEIRA" SETTLEMENT

The following testimony was given by Irma Brunetto, of the National MST Leadership, to Marta Harnecker during an interview carried out in Chapecó on May 8, 2001. Irma participated in the first occupations of land in Santa Catarina at the end of 1984 and 1985. Before that she was in the Pastoral Commission for Land, in the Movement of Women Farmers and from there she joined the MST. She was one of the Movement's organizers from the start. She was a member of the state government for three years before becoming member of the National Leadership.

The first steps

Inspiration from Ronda Alta

We had decided to prepare an occupation in Abelardo Luz, a municipality west of the State of Santa Catarina, in May 1985, but before doing so we decided to visit what the MST comrades had in Ronda Alta, Rio Grande do Sul. We didn't know how to do things. We went there to learn. They were already settled and were organized in a collective way, in groups made up of ten families. This example had a great influence on us: before carrying out occupation we had already decided to imitate them.

A group of nine young people from the Youth Pastoral of the Catholic Church camped in Abelardo Luz, and we have stayed together until today. Our group was visited by other people. They saw how we talked, how we lived, and they started approaching us.

And when, three years later, in June 1988, there was a possibility of land on Dionísio Cerqueira, we had already chosen the families that had decided to work in a collective way. We accepted going to this far-away place, close to the frontier with Argentina, because it was good land.

We were the last to be settled, but this long period of time we passed in the camp helped us know each other better, know who was really ready to work in a collective way and who wasn't, and this allowed us to be better prepared to face our new life and even create our work commissions.

From small groups to a single large one

When we got there the idea was to create small groups with ten families, like we had seen in Ronda Alta. The first thing we did was to look over the land. It had mountains, plains, land with araucarias, a very valuable tree.

When we came back from this visit we started talking about how we would distribute this land to the families, because of its irregular topography. Should we benefit some families with better land while others would receive bad land?, should we put infrastructure on some, but not on others?, why should some families be favored and others not? The irregular topography and the natural resources of the soil made us break this plan of small groups of cooperation, and we then decided to unite the 35 families from the Abelardo Luz camp in a single group.

A municipality incorporates 25 more families

Later on 25 more families from the Dionísio Cerqueira Municipality that had not participated in the struggle also joined, but this was because the mayor exerted pressure. It was one of our first fights. We could not avoid it, but we had to negotiate with the mayor and the Incra superintendent, a progressive person who even shared the idea of the importance of collective work.

We even helped choose the families because we became members of the municipality's Agrarian Council. We were called on to help decide what kind of family should be settled. The condition was that they accept the idea of collective work. You can well imagine what that meant for people who had never heard anything about agrarian reform or our Movement! That was 13 years ago.

We decided to approach those peasants, talk to them about our struggle and support them when they made up their group. We tried to win them over to our proposal because we knew that success depended to a great extent on the way they would integrate into the process. If they started to work individually, this was a menace for us, because if something happened, each one of them would claim his own piece of land.

So we established an imaginary line of division of the land and decided that some of us would work on one side and the others, on the other side. We also distributed infrastructure. We were not at all sure about what could happen with that group. We thought it would be unable to overcome difficulties. The truth is that some of those families, who had accepted the proposal for collective work only to get a piece of land quickly, started leaving. Of the 25 original families only 12 stayed on. In our group also we had some people leave. But this always happens.

Difficulties during the first years

At the beginning, during the first three years, we went through a very difficult situation, even more difficult than those three years at the camp. Sometimes we even lacked food, though we never went hungry. The land was very compact, it had been used only for cattle-raising. We only had a pair of oxen for 35 families. There were no conditions for sowing and we had no credits, but we got a loan until we were given the credit to purchase 11 cows to guarantee the milk we needed; the fertilizer so the land could be saved and start producing; and a tractor. We started making gardens and sowing rice, beans, and corn: the essential products to feed ourselves. During those first years we worked to guarantee food.

At that time, both groups were autonomous.

They do not build an *agrovila*

The way we group our houses is not like a typical *agrovila*; we decided on a geographical space for the families to build their own homes. Each chose the place where it would like to build its own house, so some were closer to each other while others were further away, but always within a definite perimeter. In the middle of the settlement we have the community center with the school, the kindergarten, the refrigerator. And some distance away there are two groups of houses. None of them is more than a five-minute walk from the other.

The families who came from the camp, we were lucky to bring with us the wood we needed to build our houses. We were camping in the woods, and had to chop down many trees to make the roads. Since the wood would be lost, we got Incra's authorization to saw

124

it up and give each family member of the camp two cubic meters. We had to transport this wood over 500 kilometers, and we used it to build our own homes using the system of mutual help – a very exceptional situation. Since we had that possibility, we left the fazenda's facilities: houses, shed, stable, for the 25 families coming from the municipality. The manager's house was very big; we housed four families there.

ORGANIZATION OF THE SETTLEMENTS

Groups of families

From the very beginning, the 35 families formed groups at the base and it was there that we first carried out discussions and then launched ideas and initiatives.

The groups of families (18) have always been the spinal column for the organization of our settlement. All work will first be discussed within these groups. If we have to mobilize them for the struggle, it is within the group that we decide how many people will go; if we have visitors, they are distributed by groups for lunch and lodging. In our groups we analyze proposals and guide the resulting actions.

We didn't have here what happens in the majority of places: that the groups of families disappear after they get to the settlement, in particular because they live far from each other.

In 1990 the MST had the idea to create militant nuclei. Their main aim was to study and go into detail of specific discussions before giving practical guidelines for the activities. Since we already had our own organized groups of families, we did not agree to create militant nuclei on top. How were we going to work in the cooperative, if some were militants and others not? The space to carry out the tasks that were being proposed for the militant nuclei was, in our opinion, the settlement's coordinating meetings, and in the assemblies with all the settlers we analysed the situation and studied specific subjects.

Our groups met every 15 days and they always had a working agenda and subjects to be discussed. Things were easier because the families lived next to one another.

In our state we have had at one time 350 groups of families.

Structure

We created a coordination or leadership for the settlement, made up of five to nine people. Then, since new tasks kept coming up, we started creating specific sectors, commissions, and only the more general aspects reached the leaders. So we have: commissions, groups for discussion, a political and social coordination and an economic coordination. When we analyze very polemic subjects that require a deeper analysis, we join both coordinations. For some time, we worked on the social, economic and political question in only one unit.

At the beginning we created several commissions: agricultural work, planning and education.

We were always very flexible in everything. We kept evolving and modifying, increasing the number of commissions, excluding some, creating others; we were never rigid.

Regulations

When we had to draft our internal regulations, we tried to follow the Ronda Alta settlement's, but they had only 10 regulations, and our reality was much more complex so we had many more things to regulate. We then decided to draft the regulations on the basis of our own needs. We put two or three people on this task. They needed about a month, then we submitted the draft to analysis within the groups and after that, we submitted it to the assembly. The regulations were for the 35 families who came from the camp. Those who came from the municipality drafted their own, and logically they needed more time for that.

Liberated cadres

We liberated some people so they could work in the Movement even before settling; that is the case of a comrade who is now in Mato Grosso. He camped with us, was settled here and is a member of the cooperative, but he moved to work in another state practically at the same time in which we settled.

At the beginning there were only three of us liberated; now we are nine in the whole settlement, which has 60 families. There was never any doubt about the importance of having liberated cadres, even if at times we have protested because of the excessive number.

At first, the contributions of the cadres liberated for the Movement to the internal work of the settlement were more intense, because we had to consolidate the whole group. I tried to divide my time, for example, between the cooperative and work outside. Now the settlement needs me less and less.

Quota of support to the MST

When we won the Procera in 1986, the Movement decided that a percentage of that credit should be given over to support the organization. If the person received 1000 reales in credit, he was committed to hand 40 to the organization. Not all states have the same percentages; some contribute 3%, others 5%. Each state defines the quota according to the reality of its own region. Not everyone agreed with this. Many people joined the MST to conquer land and once they had it, they didn't want to have anything more to do with it. When I joined, for example, that was my only aim: land. Then my head started changing, but that doesn't happen to everyone. This matter of handing in 4% of each credit is a collective decision, adopted in an assembly of our settlements. Even if it isn't accepted by everyone, if the majority decides to pay, one must pay to be able to stay in the Movement. If someone does not agree he must leave. This measure was used by the media in their campaign against us; they said we forced them to pay.

UNIFICATION PROCESS

Need made us jump

The unification of the two groups that made up our settlement started little by little. At the beginning both groups had their own coordinations. Once a month we met and exchanged experiences, helping each other. We started working together in some aspects of the community, such as the school. Then it was need itself that made us jump.

A process helped along by solidary gestures

In 1990 we decided to create a cooperative while the other group stayed on as an informal group. Even though we had thought about the convenience of unifying, conditions were still unripe and it was not convenient to force the process. We decided, however, that all benefits earned through the cooperative would be distributed on an equal basis between both groups, even if they were not partners. That was very important, because if we had received benefits while they didn't, there would have been differences and we didn't want that.

The following year, we took a month-long course to study the possibility of unifying in the future. We even planted a tree as symbol of our unification. It was a very interesting process!

Then we started discussing the things in which we could start unifying. In production, we began with apiculture, which was the simplest of them all; then structures, the shed, the warehouses, part of the land; cattle were last. We went from the simple to the more complex. One year we unified one thing; the next year, another thing. In 1995 the other group finally joined the cooperative as partner. We created a single general leadership and a single coordination, and everyone joined the work commissions. For example, in the group in charge of work in the field, there were people from here and there. It was a very detailed, slow, process, step by step, so as not to destroy the work carried out during all those years.

What contributed most to this unification process was our attitude with the other group. After having rejected them in the first place because we wanted to fill empty posts with families from our own settlement (19), when their integration in our settlement was final we then decided to change our attitude and accept them, attract them to our Movement and help them become integrated.

We tried to go very slowly in this unification, hoping the process would ripen little by little, avoiding any pressure. Several people, who came to visit us and saw that there were two groups, insisted that we had to unify them; they didn't understand what we were waiting for before unifying.

We had a lot of criticism during this process. At the beginning, when we had unified some activities only, we tended to give priority to each group's activity rather than to common activities. That was when we began to realize that we had to unify everything, otherwise we would run the risk of falling backward. Today our unity is such that it would seem we had never worked separately.

PRODUCTION

Our first planning

Our group was created with a lot of courage, a lot of effort; we had no examples to copy. I remember that it was very difficult to do our first planning, because our group was very big in relation to other experiences within the Movement. We asked some agronomists to come and help us but they knew even less than we did. When the time came to find solutions, we had to do everything according to our own opinion, nobody could decide for us.

We tried to study how much we had to plant each of potatoes, onions, in relation to our own needs. Since we had never done this, it was very slow going until we hit on the correct numbers: sometimes we produced more than we needed, at others we came short of some product. We have been at this for 12 years, and only three years ago did we start to produce according to our needs for survival. Today we know what each family consumes.

At the beginning, we used to market two things mainly: mate and beans. We had 10 000 plants of mate and produced around 300 tons, giving us an important income. We produced corn, but it was only for ourselves, rarely did we sell it.

Planning for eight years

Later on we planned for eight years. We studied our progress and how far we could go, and we carried it out. In our settlement, food, survival always comes first. What we wanted with planning was for the people to have a good life, to eat well and all that. But people have other needs besides food, and you have to try to satisfy them. That is when we started looking for ways to generate more income to satisfy them.

After some time, we defined our lines of production. Today we invest more in those areas where we get larger incomes, such as the production of chicken, milk, fish and mate.

Chicken production

Initially a small undertaking

We have chicken agro-industrial production; it started when we created our cooperative.

We started out with a small experience. We prepared a project for an 8 by 12 meter structure. The idea was to have something to eat and sell surplus production. We could produce 1000, consume 500 and sell the rest to buy another lot of chicks. That body financed a credit that we later paid back. Then we started selling our surplus in the city, and it was always very well received. They fought over who would buy our chickens. We sold them for many years without complying with the regulations, without making our marketing legal. Now everything is legal.

Food

Chickens eat a mixture of our corn and our soy, but we also depend on the purchase of some ingredients to prepare the mixture. We must also buy the chicks, and this makes us dependant. And we must purchase medicine, vitamins. Our chicken is of a better quality, heavier; we raise them for two months approximately, whereas other agro-industries only raise them for around 40 days. We have been in this production for the past eight or ten years.

Marketing

At the beginning they came to buy the chicken in the settlement but later we began taking them to market, without any trade name, just the package. And people from Argentina came to buy them; they represented our biggest demand for this high-quality product.

Today it is an important activity; we have refrigeration for 7000 chickens a day. So far we are using 15% of this capacity. In five years we will need 52 chicken breeding structures. Today we have only 12; we need 40 more.

We have the labor force to work the cold-storage plant: the settled families, but we don't have enough raw material or the conditions to build those 40 structures we need to breed chicken. We are thinking of solving this through integration: buying the chickens from an outside farmer and slaughter them ourselves. But this means, among other things, that we have to create conditions for that farmer to breed his chickens: we must produce the mixture they eat and give him technical assistance. It is a huge challenge, because it is a very complex activity, but it is profit-making. Our major incomes come from chickens.

Credits require technology way above our needs

We were very aware that we didn't need such a huge cold-storage plant, but the law requires at least that to be able to enter into the market. It is a method to benefit large agro-industries. The small ones have no possibilities at all. In order to get federal approval – the CIF – and sell in Paraná and Argentina, which are our natural markets, we were required to have at least that.

The credit was given by Procera. (20) They allowed us to go a little over the limit to install the cold-storage plant. It cost us around 300 000 *reais*. This year, the third after we were given the credit, we have to start paying it back. If we don't pay our debts we will be assigned no more credits. The MST is trying to negotiate all the debts together, but if it is unsuccessful we shall have to get the money for the monthly payments from the cold-storage plant's income.

The cooperative

Our cooperative is greatly in debt with the government. The debts are several years old, they have already been postponed. Our income is enough for our survival, but we have been unable so far to accumulate a reserve of money to pay the debt. This is one of the great difficulties of all cooperatives, not just ours, and it is related with the crisis in agriculture, because today, products like corn, beans etc. have very low prices and the income we get from their sale is not enough.

We must also recall that the cooperatives answer not only the personal needs of the families, but also a series of social needs. An example of this is that our cooperative provides all the school material for children up to second grade (21); it also covers transportation and health expenses etc.

On the other hand, when a member is seriously sick, the cooperative pays part of the expenses. We have no social security, but we have some norms: if the person has a mild disease – toothache, headache, diarrhea – he loses his salary for that day. But if his disease is serious, if he has to be hospitalised, the workdays justified by the doctor are paid as though he were working.

The cooperative also contributes to the payment of medicines. When a person has to have a continuous treatment – for example, for high blood pressure – the cooperative pays half the price of the medicine.

The cooperative, inspired in Cuban CPAs, gave a legal personality to what we already had: a group for collective work. Only the legal part changed. It implied more work than what we would have had if we had remained an informal group, but at the same time it gave us more security as far as capital and investments is concerned. Because in the past, capital, tractors, were registered in the name of two or three people, and the same was true for bank accounts, the list of payments for the products handed out by the government – which the peasant needs to pay his taxes. And that is a huge risk, because some day these people may change their attitude and harm the whole collective.

This method brought more security from a legal point of view: now the common patrimony is in the name of the cooperative, and if someone decides to leave it he won't harm the rest of the people. This is an advantage. Another aspect is that we were forced to improve our organization because of accounting requirements and many other things. What did not change with the creation of the cooperative was the logic of our leadership. The disadvantage is that there are many more requirements from an administrative point of view, bureaucracy grows and there are legal deviations.

Bureaucratization

There are laws the cooperative must comply with: "you can do this, you can't do that" and this somehow has made our leaders bureaucrats. Many mass leaders are completely absorbed by work in the cooperatives and don't have much time left for other things. There is a concrete need, someone must answer for it. We should look for another kind of cadre for this task.

Many people believe the cooperatives have made the Movement bureaucratic. I think this has a lot to do with the methods used, with the way planning is carried out and all that.

In our case, it is clear that today, after having formed the cooperative, we have much more bureaucratic work than before to act according to the law, but at the same time these legal requirements force us to improve our organization. And even so, in spite of all these requirements, we have had problems; we need more control and a series of other things.

Trade Cooperatives

I believe things change much more when we create trade cooperatives.

There were several settlements in the region, but none, except ours, produced in a collective way. Then we saw the need to look for another formula for cooperation in order to link them, so we came up with the idea of a Regional Trade Cooperative (Cooperoeste). Thanks to it we began to develop this experience with the associations in milk production. We built three small units for the milk and cheese industry in the region, and later on, on July 20, 1996, we created the São Miguel D'Oeste – Santa Catarina cooperative. In most places, first they constitute the cooperative and then they organize their capital, their production. Here it was different. When you create the regional cooperative you are taking a major step in industry. Today there is long-life milk, which implies bigger investments both for the settlers and the small farmers.

We sell the milk to that cooperative, which sends it to the factory in another municipality, about 60 kilometers away from our place. The trademark is *Terra Viva* and it is being distributed throughout the whole state. The factory works with our milk as well as with the milk from the other settlements in the region – there are 13, with about 500 families – and that of the small farmers.

Toxics for agriculture

We always worry not to contaminate the water and all that. At the beginning we had a very nice analysis and came to the conclusion that we must never use poison, that we must protect the waters, the woods, but when we decided to plant tobacco – because the price of corn and beans had really gone down – everything was forgotten. That was in 1991. We had to solve an economic problem. At that time we had no agro-industry, we still didn't have cattle for milk. Tobacco – very income-yielding at that time – solved our immediate problem to earn money.

We then decided to produce tobacco and we started to use poison. Then we stopped producing tobacco, but we continued using toxics for agriculture in the rest of our production. It is a very complicated matter. We are searching for alternatives, but we still use poison and so far we are unable to stop. This is our great contradiction.

Even if we know they are harmful, we use them because it is more practical. It is not safer or more economic, but it saves a lot of labor force. Instead of cleaning the land, for example, we fumigate with poison that dries everything up, so it is unnecessary to hoe the land; then we plant, fumigate with another product to stop wild grass from growing. People can then devote themselves to other activities; you don't need so many people for that work.

For economic reasons we destroyed a whole project. But the worst thing was that this did not help us solve our economic problem either. It was the greatest error we made during the life of our cooperative. It provided no income since we became indebted because of a whole structure we had to build, and tobacco did not give us the expected results. We became intoxicated and we intoxicated the land, because the poisons are very strong. We still have debts. We have had to pay a very high price for this error.

We are aware of the problem with toxics for agriculture, but it will not be easy to stop using them. We can't eliminate them completely overnight. To use organic fertilizers, for example, you require about four or five years. We shall have to advance little by little until we are able to work without them, but we are convinced that it is possible, and we are doing our best.

School

Interest over the school from the very beginning

We settled in June 1988 and from that moment on we began struggling to have a school. In 1989 it started to function. And we then looked for teachers friendly to agrarian reform and willing to work on the MST's proposal. There was no one with these characteristics. We finally found a woman teacher who knew nothing about the Movement but who was willing, open, and wanted to learn. Today she is at the faculty in Ijuí, belongs to the first group called Teaching for Land, and is an active member of the cooperative. Later on we got another woman teacher. So now we have two.

Our school has worked with Paulo Freire's method from the very beginning, and it constitutes a national point of reference.

The students study until the fourth series (22) in the cooperative, then go on to another school 20 kilometers away. Then they must go on to second grade (23) in the city, 35 kilometers away. Or they study in Veranópolis, or in another place. All this is paid for by the cooperative: school material, and though the office of the mayor is in charge of transportation, sometimes it has no resources and we have to pay for it because it is a commitment made by the cooperative.

School: one more cooperative

In school, children are organized like adults: they hold assemblies, have work groups, and commissions. It is called Cooperative School. (24)

Kindergartens or *Cirandas*

At the beginning women didn't work. Our group was made up

of 18 single men and 17 married ones, mostly young men, and they believed that if women also worked they would lose out because they would have to pay the women for their work.

During our second year women started working and then the idea came up for the rotation in the care of the children. This formula went on for about three years.

After this, these three groups united in a single *ciranda*. (25)

Young people don't want to work the land

The problem of young people is very difficult. When they leave our schools in the settlements and go to the cities to continue their studies – they are then 10 or 11 years old – they start falling under other influences, mainly consumer attitudes. Even if everyone here has a television set, it is not the same to see something on the screen than to live together with city people. Fashion comes into their life and all that. What a terrible thing! They start dreaming about other things and come under other influences. And when they go on to second grade, this influence is much stronger.

The huge majority of young people, especially young girls, don't like to work in the countryside; they prefer to be domestic help in the cities. For these girls, it is a punishment to work under the sun hoeing the land, planting; they don't consider this work valuable. Very few of these girls stay on in the countryside. Some are in Movement schools, in Iterra, for example; some married militants, but in general they don't value the cooperative's efforts for their training. They just finish their studies and go away. This is very frustrating for those of us who are older. Young men see this a little differently, a little better. Fifty percent of them don't plan on staying on in the cooperative. One of their reasons is that here in the cooperative they don't get enough according to their dreams, which are different from ours; they want to consume, have fun, go out and all that. One of our huge worries is this matter related to young people.

The Movement mobilizes many young people for the

occupations, but the children of the settlers don't have the same enthusiasm.

The critical situation agriculture is going through is throwing young people out of the countryside, and we have not been spared. An option would be for them to go to the camps, but something interesting happens: their own parents, who went through this experience, don't want their children to go there.

Recreation: a productive task

We always put in the first place tasks related to education, health, sports, and recreation, which we consider a productive task. The cooperative pays for the hours invested in building the football field as though they had been worked in the fields.

On womem

We thought our collective group was going to solve the problems related to women, because they were oppressed as a result of individual property, but experience proved this was not the case. It was our great discovery: cooperation alone does not solve the problem related to women's participation. There is a material condition that helps – collective property. The cooperative is a solution for women's productive work, but not for housework. Their house, their world, cleaning chores, the well-being of their families... that problem is not solved. Sometimes women don't participate in a meeting because they have to make bread. We had to draft regulations that stated, for example, that bread is less important than a meeting, and if women are absent from the meeting they will lose their rights. Both men and women have to have a justified cause for their absence.

The collective aspect of our work has to be a permanent subject for us.

There is something else: during the day we have kindergartens, but not at night, so if there is some activity in the evening we have to discuss with the families which of the two parents will participate.

Our cooperatives and the MST must carry out a much deeper analysis of family relations, how relations between men and women should be so women can also be free.

On the other hand, there are women who are not interested in freeing themselves, they invent anything at all so they won't have to participate; nothing can be done with them. In our cooperative we have made some progress in the division of tasks related to the family, all the men have housework to do: on weekends they sweep, cook... Women still work more than men, though we have made a lot of progress in this anyhow. But sometimes it is the women themselves who keep back: the husband tells her to go to the meeting, that he will stay home, but she still doesn't go. What can you do with this attitude?

We must work more on this aspect; women must discover the need to participate. Of course, it is much better to stay home when it rains, for women finally have what they always dreamed of: they have a husband, they have children, they have a home, they have land, the cooperative solves countless problems they had to overcome in the past.

Some settlements have a collective dining room, we are thinking of creating our own, but in the beginning we were unable to because of economic reasons, then it became increasingly difficult because people like being at home. On the other hand, we also believe it is important for families to have a little privacy, even though from an economic point of view, a collective dining room would be the best thing.

What happens is that the majority of women work only half a day. The cold-storage plant has two shifts: one in the morning and one in the afternoon, and the women can decide if they will work half a shift or a whole one. The collective dining room could be more necessary if they worked a whole shift.

Relations with the municipality

Our group was related to the PT (26) and the union from the time it was camped. The first thing we did when we came to the Dionísio Cerqueira settlement was to join in the life of the municipality, the union, see how the Party Worked.

We had already organized ourselves within the settlement and we had decided that some of our settlers would give priority to union activities; others, to those of the party, and still others to the Movement's.

The union was a yellow one (27) and it had had the same leaders for the past 15 years. We then started looking for outstanding leaders within the municipality, the pastoral, and we contributed to change this situation. In the beginning it was very difficult, the police followed us because landless people had a negative reputation.

It was through the union that we participated in the life of the municipality. In 1990 there were union elections, and the statute they had practically prevented anyone from winning them. People had lost interest in participating in the union, they were not stimulated. We then decided to call a meeting to change the statutes. Practically the whole settlement participated, 60 families. We got a bus to travel; we were more than a 100 people. We were thus a majority at the assembly, and we were able to change the statute, so in the following elections we won. The displaced leaders tried to throw justice against us, but after two long years justice recognized us. This victory in the union was something very important for us. Ninety percent of the merit went to our settlement.

At that time unionism was well seen, the union movement had a combative spirit, and it was important to head a union in the municipality.

Two years later, in the 1992 municipal elections – the first elections of this kind in which we participated – we elected our own candidate to councilman. The first councilman in the history of the PT municipality came from our settlement. His mandate was fantastic, very combative; it had class. Even if he was the only leftist councilman, he hit the right harshly and became a point of reference within the municipality. His good work and our support contributed a lot to the PT's victory in the 1996 elections for mayor.

The right wing said that if that candidate won the elections, he would work in favor of the settlement, and the rest of the people would have no rights. It tried to put the community in the municipality against us, but this didn't work because we won. And now, in the year 2000, we elected the mayor once again, and our councilman has started on his third mandate.

We stand out not only in politics; we are also municipal football champions.

We have also opened new doors in trade. At present we are well taken into account, we have no problems to buy on credit. During these past 15 years there has never been a complaint against us, and our problems have been solved among ourselves.

One day, the city judge went to the settlement to learn about our internal regulations, to find out why we never called on the police for anything, why we never recurred to the law. He wanted to understand our secret.

We have made several donations of food. The last time we had a campaign, we donated food for the kindergartens in the city, we sent them baskets with all our products.

We think our insistence in having a mayor from the PT has been very positive. Today we participate in the Municipal Council for Health; in the Municipal Council for Education – our woman teacher participates there and she has been able to take our teaching method to other schools. We also have a member in the Council for Rural Development, we have people in the union, and we try to participate at all levels.

But this doesn't mean everything is perfect. We were very much affected by the strong campaign the right had launched against us when it said that the mayor would benefit the settlement only; he tried to prove this wasn't true and we suffered the consequences. He takes care of the settlement in the last place. For example, during the first mandate our roads were terrible, and we were the last to be heard. We had 4 unpaved kilometers, and each time they came to see us they told us: "How can this happen if you have a mayor from the PT? You must occupy the mayor's office." The mayor never helped us finance a bus to go anywhere – for example, to a mobilization. We never create trouble for this, but we do have our needs that are not answered, that could be placed on their priority list.

Thanks to the work of the PT, the municipality improved in many aspects – for example, in health. But there is another problem: since there is a coalition with other parties, the Department of Education did nothing new during its first mandate, nothing at all! Nothing! Only now is it able to do something. The PT should consider the Department of Education a strategic front and not give it over to the PMDB (28), because ideological aspects are very important to us. What happens is that the Department of Public Works is much more in the public eye and they believe this is important to renew their mandate. They are more immersed in winning than in ideological debate.

In Chapecó, for example, they have invested a lot in education, and are interested in creating programs to work on this matter. In Dionísio Cerqueira they have given much more attention to a correct management than to investments in management. The difference with previous administrations resides in honesty, in a good management of resources, in good roads.

We participate in our budget, but since our resources are scarce this is not very meaningful.

Evaluation of the MST

Right now we are analysing our limitations. The way our people are reacting against the government's offensive has made us see our weak points within the Movement.

Some people think that everything we have done is wrong. I don't agree with this analysis: we have built many valuable things during these past 15 years. The MST has become a sort of state. We are doing what the state should do, and much more. The Movement worries about the human being as a whole. We fight for the land, the home, the community, education, health, culture, women, young people… In all Brazil there is no other organization working on all these things. While guiding the struggle, we must think about the school, the teaching method, the woman teacher, the student, art, music… It has to do with an incredible amount of complex things. That is why I always say that we are like a state. I believe we have been building a huge thing.

Everyone knows us already. We organize ourselves; we occupy land, a public lot. Now we must modify what we do, we must create different things to fight this model.

The other thing that happened is that we grew a lot and were greatly praised – we are considered "the light of the world", "the light of Brazil" – so we became very enthused with all this and we left some doors open. Now we have discovered that one of our great problems is the limited awareness of our people as far as being an exploited class is concerned. They understand perfectly well that they must fight for better economic conditions, for credits, but not for a new society.

IV – General considerations

After these concrete experiences, we now go on to explain in detail the teachings the MST obtained from them and from many others throughout Brazil.

THE STRUGGLE DOES NOT END WITH THE CONQUEST OF THE LAND

The different experiences of agrarian reform as practiced not only in Brazil but in many other parts of the world prove – as we have already said – that it is not enough to assign the peasants the land to work on; at the same time conditions for his work must be created to allow him to survive: without machinery, seeds, credits, technical know-how to benefit from the progress made by the technological revolution, without marketing outlets for their products, instead of becoming a space for freedom, the land becomes a nightmare and they end up selling it at very low prices, or simply abandoning it.

The struggle doesn't end with the conquest of the land, that being only the first step to reach the other aims; only a global transformation of society will allow that. Meanwhile we must plan and organize production to guarantee the survival of the families already settled and to promote, whenever possible, "the social and economic development of the peasants who conquer the land." (29) This is not an easy task, since often the lands assigned are low quality, exhausted or weakened because the large landowners have not used them correctly. On the other hand, these lands usually have a very poor infrastructure, and as we have already seen, the government doesn't guarantee any, nor the adequate means of production, nor inputs or regular technical assistance, leaving the peasant abandoned to his own fate. (30)

It is therefore very important for the peasants who have already conquered their land to assume this new struggle successfully, to stay within the Movement in an organized and articulated way. (31)

ORGANIZATION OF THE SETTLED COMMUNITY

The MST believes the peasants must stay within the settlements organized in groups of families just as they were while they were camping. To contribute to this it has encouraged the creation of small rural communities, trying to concentrate their homes: the so-called *agrovilas*. But this guideline has been followed successfully only in a small number of settlements.

Their materialization has depended on the characteristics of the different regions of the country, and the degree of political awareness reached by the families. There are regions like the Northeast where the peasants have always been organized in towns, instead of putting their homes on their respective lots of land. This has to do in the first place with the characteristics of the soil in that region. This one is not very productive: it is a semiarid place where we can't have kitchen gardens and forces the rural worker to go out to places relatively far away from his home, to do his agricultural work. For this worker it was natural to fight so the state would build *agrovilas*. There it is the objective situation that makes this necessary. But the same is not true in the South, where the land is much more productive. There the trend is to live on your own lot of land. (32) On the other hand, since the idea of the *agrovilas* was forcefully imposed there by Incra in the 80s, they generated a lot of resistance.

In that region, *agrovilas* have been created only where there were groups who worked the land in a collective way and had established agricultural and cattle-breeding cooperatives.

Besides Incra's compulsive policy, there are two other reasons why the peasant from the South refuses to live in an *agrovila:* on the one hand, the important distance there is usually between his home and the lot he works; and on the other, the little space between one house and the other, that does not allow for a garden or animal husbandry.

And since the MST can guide but not impose the way in which houses are distributed, it has had to accept a mixed solution: some families go to the *agrovilas* and others stay on their individual lots. (34)

But the fact that the majority of families have decided to build their house on their lot has been an obstacle to organization and community life: the distances are huge and usually they have not planned for spaces to gather all of the settled families.

That is why the MST is experimenting at present with some kind of design for the location of the houses, which will take into account the peasant's ancestral wish to place his house on his own lot and at the same time keep the houses close to one another. (35)

From the experiences carried out in Rondonia, Mato Grosso do Sul and Espírito Santo, they are already planning a new way to organize the houses, called *Núcleos de Moradia* and *Núcleos Habitacionais*.

Núcleos de moradia

In the so-called *Núcleos de Moradia*, the homes of the settlers are built on the lot itself, which usually has 25 hectares. Previously, though, they have decided on a parcelling system that allows the houses to be close to one another. Let us imagine the sun and its rays, all converging toward a central space, where there is a common area. The houses are placed around the sun. With this design, from 10 to 15 families can gather, and if the lot is smaller then up to 20 to 25. The design must guarantee that the families will build their homes according to a specific previously – agreed-upon alignment. (36)

Núcleo habitacional

This experience of *Núcleos Habitacionais* has been developed in Espírito Santo. In this case too, they are small groups of families that build their homes close to each other, each lot having approximately half a hectare. The main difference with respect to the other experience is that the homes are not built on the lots themselves. After a topographical study of the land, the families decide where they want to place the *Núcleo Habitacional*, and they prepare a design that will put the homes close to each other, on a roadside, for example, and then the lots are assigned as close to their respective homes as possible. The only requirement is to put the homes close to each other – the rest is up to the group of families' imagination.

In the first as well as in the second case, the design of the lots and the spaces between the homes tries to bring the homes near each other while taking into account other technical aspects, such as the topography, water sources, streets, electric network etc.

In both cases they create a small social area, in the central space of the group of homes or at one end, where they can build a hall for meetings and parties, a small shed to store agricultural and sport products, a school and a place for religious ceremonies. (37) The social area is strategically important because what they pursue when they bring the homes closer to each other is mainly to create conditions for closer social interrelations and, from there, establish different ways for the families to cooperate.

Agrovilas in the Nort and the Nordheast

In the North and the Northeast they are working with two kinds of *agrovilas*. The first kind groups all of the settlement's families in a single *agrovila*, about 500 to 600 families. They haven't studied their results yet. In the second kind, they divide the settlement's families in several smaller *agrovilas*. There is an experience in Sergipe, where the settlement's 700 families were grouped in 34 *agrovilas* with about 20 homes each. The lots were 25 by 40 meters. In this settlement they implanted an irrigation project that allowed the families to have a certain amount of irrigated hectares (four per family) so their homes were placed near those areas, and that is why some *agrovilas* are very close to each other, sometimes you only have to cross the street. But each one has its own internal organization.

Experience has shown that the *agrovilas* made up by 40 to 150 homes have the best conditions for their organization, and to solve problems of the infrastructure like water, electricity and streets, even if still in a somewhat rustic way. This doesn't mean there aren't any *agrovilas* that work very well with 25 families, but so far it is evident that less than 25 families or more than 150 makes organization more difficult. (38)

In order to distribute the land in the most coherent way according to their aims, in some places, like Espírito Santo, the MST has been able to organize a topography undertaking that participates in Incra's bidding for this work. (39)

Groups of settlements

On the other hand, while it is very important for the consolidation of the MST's aims to create groups of families in the settlements, it is also important to constitute what some call *pólos de assentamentos* (settlement concentrations). An isolated settlement, surrounded by latifundia, will hardly have any impact and all its efforts to reach the market with a minimum of possibilities tend to fail. To change the system's logic in some aspects – in particular by pushing the idea of creating a popular alternative market with products from the MST's agricultural cooperatives – it is essential to gather many settlements in one zone, and create the kind of articulation that will multiply their impact in the region, both in the economic and the educational, cultural and political spheres.

In Rio Grande do Sul they are working on the idea of gathering from 1000 to 1500 families settled in a rather limited perimeter, so their economic and political impact will be much stronger. Small isolated settlements end up unable to alter the logic of the region, and they are swallowed up by it. (40)

The concentration of several settlements in only one group also helps solve problems of the infrastructure, since it is not the same thing to build a road and bring water to a settlement made up of only 20 families, than to do all this for 1500 families. For this it is

148

very important to carry out political and ideological work in the region, so its union and political leaders and the local administrations are won over to the project. And it is even more important that the neighbors of the region have a friendly attitude to the MST proposals. A local radio station is essential too in order to have direct communication with the people of the region.

Raffle by groups of families

In all previous experiences analysed, we have seen that the key to success is the organization in groups of families; so it is essential that from the camp itself they be grouped by affinities, and then be present as a group at the raffle, so once they have received the land they will be able to be together in the same locality. Later they can organize an internal raffle among these families to assign each of them a specific lot.

"In the regions where we are better organized, they accept our criteria of selection. In other regions where we are weaker, Incra chooses the families, without taking into account if they had been camped or not, but in general it is the Movement's opinion that prevails." (41)

Kinds of property titles

The MST believes it is necessary to fight for legal regulations to guarantee that the land already conquered will really belong to those who are willing to work it, and not to those who want to trade with it, because there are people who register for a piece of land, not to make it produce but to sell it, make money and go settle somewhere else – usually in the city – and that is why it believes land should not be assigned as a piece of individual private property. Rather, there should be a title of concession for use of the land – which means the right of that family or group of families and their children to use and benefit from the land. This legal document guarantees possession, not property, and that is why if some families

149

are no longer interested in working the land they were assigned, they cannot sell it, they have to hand it to another peasant willing to work it. The peasant who gives up will receive the value of everything he has built on his lot, with his own and his family's efforts, but he will get nothing for the land itself, because it is considered a gift of nature.

Incra, on the contrary, proposes giving a property title already during the second year, after the legal process of censing the families has started, together with the Authorization of Occupation (42) and the Charter of Acceptance (43). The idea is that the peasant receive his title as soon as possible (which he will be unable to transfer for ten years), together with his payments card so he will be able to reimburse Incra for the expenses it has had to create the settlement.

The MST also favors the assignment of collective titles where the group of families is willing to work collectively. And in this case and that of individual titles it believes that both the man and woman's names must be inscribed in them. This implies some advantages for the woman, since she is then considered a worker with equal rights with man (vacations, pension and other benefits).

Groups of families in the settlements

Whatever the way in which land is distributed, what the MST stresses is the creation of groups of families. They can be territorial groups – like the case of the *Núcleos de Moradia* or *Núcleos Habitacionais* – but what can happen is that larger communities, more than 30 families, require that two or more groups of families be created. These groups are the basic instance for the settlement's management. (44)

Experience has made the MST believe that the best thing is for each group of families to choose among its members, two coordinators: a man and a woman, so the feminine vision of things will be present in discussions and coordinations for the settlements.

Another lesson learned after years of activity is the need to

150

avoid excessive assemblies, because it is very difficult to have profound discussions. And assemblies can also be manipulated by any president in power.

That is why it believes it is essential that discussions and decisions be held in smaller groups, like the groups of families, where everyone can express his opinion, and ideas and proposals be seriously analysed. Assemblies must be to submit proposals from these smaller groups. So the MST recommends the holding of "mini assemblies" by community. (46)

For the debate to be fruitful, there has to be good previous information on the matters up for debate. As Aristobulo Isturiz, ex mayor of Caracas, says, "There is no democracy without well-informed people." And if there are different proposals, it is also essential to have really lofty debates that will respect everyone's ideas.

ORGANIZATION OF SERVICES

Internal services

To avoid the interference within the settlements of unknown people who often are against the MST – for example, the owner of a small shop, the garage man, the mechanic and others – the Movement suggests that at the camp they already study how to solve these services with people from the settlement itself – creating, for example, a community market managed by nuclei at the base or by the settlement's coordinators.

It also recommends that the coordination of activities related to the gas station, internal transportation and other services be taken over by the settlement's coordinators.

If there is a service cooperative in the region, it could take over these activities.

They can also discuss with the families the possibility of organizing a work cooperative with people from the settlement, which would not only build houses but also take over other services for all the settlers. (47)

Education

From the camp itself they must prepare the work group for education, with one or two people by group of families, to cooperate with the school and participate in the analysis of the teaching plan.

The settlements must try to guarantee that the school be built within the settlement itself with teachers who will implement the teaching guidelines of the MST. (48) This is the Movement's struggle, because very often the mayors would prefer sending means of transportation so the students can go to municipal schools.

They must also try to create a kindergarten for children from 0 to 6 years old in order to train them from the very beginning in community life and create conditions for women to be able to work.

It is also very convenient to organize a library to stimulate reading, putting in one single hall the MST materials and the magazines collected, so they will be available to the families.

Healt

Health has been from the very beginning one of the MST's concerns, even though the Health Sector as such was born only four years ago. (49) We have already seen testimonies about the way in which the Movement assumes these tasks.

Social infrastructure

We have also seen the importance of having a social center, where the families can gather to have fun, hold their celebrations and cultural activities, religious ceremonies etc. It is also important to have a small square, a football field, a park for children, and nice gardens.

Religion

Since the majority of the peasants are believers and belong to different religions or sects, it is important to stimulate their contents leading to freedom, and encourage a universal feeling among the practitioners. (50)

If there are several religions, it is advisable for them to unite and build a place for their cults, whose use would be programmed by mutual agreement.

Embellishing the area

The physical aspect of the communities is very important. Beautiful gardens, streets with names of fighters from the people themselves, clean and cared-for areas, reforestation with native plants – all this creates a nice atmosphere. In the case of the *agrovilas* or *núcleos de moradia* or *habitacionais,* the houses must be built on the same level, and they should be painted the same color; they should also have similar fences, their agricultural structures and facilities should be well indicated, and if possible, each house should have a flag of the MST, either painted or made out of cloth.

The places that are part of the history of struggle for the land of the community should also be prominent (the first place they occupied, where they offered resistance to the police etc.), with a small monument or a simple plaque to keep the memory of the event alive.

They must also try to recover their peasant traditions, like harvest celebrations.

It is important to organize within the municipality, frequent fairs – either weekly or less frequent ones.

Stimulating actions of solidarity

Stimulating actions of solidarity with the camps of the region and nearby towns through donations of products for their schools and hospitals and voluntary work for different activities creates awareness in the people.

Organize artistic and cultural shows

One of the major problems in the settlements is lack of recreation, and this affects women and young people in particular. They have to encourage creativity to carry out different cultural activities: poetry and music festivals; using typical feasts to plan activities, organize theatre groups, musical groups, choruses, literary workshops etc.

It would be ideal to get loudspeakers and organize a community radio station, promoting young people's participation in the more important tasks.

Striving for an ecological agricultural development

While the MST is fighting for the human development of the settlers, it also strives to preserve nature.

"For us, the settlement is a rebirth of human life and of nature – says Gilmar Mauro, one of the MST's national leaders. That is why it is essential to define a policy for economic, social and human development, preserve the environment, recover river sources, replant devastated areas, avoid fires, collect garbage, avoid the use of poisons and chemical fertilizers, produce all kinds of fruit and flowers, and protect birds and wild animals." (51)

Proposals for the environment

In areas occupied by landless people and made into settlements, we must try to implement an integral rural development, understood as "a process of permanent improvement in material living conditions (food, health, housing, clothing, transportation), besides housing, cultural and spiritual conditions for all the settlers and the community they live in." (52)

On the other hand, in this integral rural development, besides aiming at the full social and human development of the rural worker and his family by eliminating all kinds of exploitation, the MST proposes the rational use of available natural resources in areas of agrarian reform, avoiding the ravage of the land.

This concern is translated in the following guidelines:

– Avoid ravaging practices of natural resources (land, water, fauna and flora) and use conservation techniques.

– Preserve the forests, defining the practice of collective use of forest species and the flora existing in the settlements, draft plans for reforestation within the settlements, to be carried out according to each one's needs.

– Develop the awareness of the need to apply a correct environmental policy in all educational and training activities.

– Promote agreements with environmental bodies to increase knowledge about this subject and develop common programs.

– Demand that the state develop public policies to support environmental protection programs, including reforestation, the preservation of natural resources and the production of agricultural and cattle-raising technologies that will not affect nature.

– Defend the boundaries of all indigenous areas, and what is left of old *quilombos* (53), and respect their culture as well.

– Fight against the use of agricultural toxic products that attempt on the life of the people and nature, by using alternative technologies for production and the control of insects and harmful weeds.

ORGANIZATION OF PRODUCTION

Guidelines in the sphere of production and cooperation
Taking into account accumulated experience, the MST has planned the following guidelines in the field of production. (54)

Plan for production
It is essential to plan production correctly, drafting a plan that will take into account the following factors: the productive potential of the different soils of the area, the climate of the region, the water available on the expropriated *fazenda*. They must also take into account the basic food needed by the settled families: they must

foresee the individual or collective production of different cereals, the breeding of animals for meat, milk, eggs, cheese, fat and different species of fruit according to the season of the year.

This production for survival must be combined with some kind of production for the local and regional markets, so each family will have a minimum income to purchase what it needs, besides the food it produces. That is why it is very important to study the potential of the local market: what products could be sold in the municipalities of the region, and how to make a better use of the conditions of the settlement. They will probably have to discuss the collective use of several facilities.

The important thing is to start creating in the people the habit of thinking in a collective way and adapt each individual dream to the existing potential for production and the real need to plan economic actions. (55)

When planning for production, environmental aspects must also be taken into account.

Forms of cooperation

Things are made much easier if you are able to have the groups of families live close to each other. Different forms of cooperation come up naturally among them, both to solve social problems and to assume together some of their economic needs (renting or purchasing machinery, transporting products to market etc.), or productive tasks, until in some cases they come to the complete collective development of their economic activities.

It is important to define while still in the camp the readiness of the groups of families to work collectively, because this must be included in the way land will be assigned and in the production plans that will be drafted.

It is possible to plan different activities of collective work that will employ young people and women – a small production of preserves, for example, bread and other similar products.

You can go from the simplest to the more complex forms of cooperation.

Technical advising group

The MST believes it is very important for the technical advising group to be convinced of the Movement's proposal to organize the settlements and cooperate for this proposal to come to life. The ideal thing is for a multidisciplinary group to live in the settlement and participate fully in its life. (56)

Credit control

It is very important for the settlers to use the credits they get to implement the economic and social proposals they have decided to push forward, as a result of the collective planning previous to their settlement, to avoid the misuse of public resources. (57)

A new way of production

The Movement strives to encourage a new way of production that will substitute the model based just on profits and ruled by the laws of the market, which concentrates on monoculture and the use of agricultural toxic products. A new model whose main aim would not be to compete in the market but to develop a more ecologic way of production that would take into account the need of the settled families and look for an alternative popular market, where it would sell its products at prices convenient for the popular sectors.

THE MST AND ALTERNATIVE TECHNOLGIES

Recently, a growing number of agronomists, technicians and farmers are looking for alternative technologies because they refuse imported technologies applied in Brazil in its process to update agriculture, which has implied the violent arrival of multinational capital and the introduction of an industrialized technological pattern based on chemical products: fertilizers, insecticides, herbicides; genetic products: hybrid seeds; and mechanical products: harvesters, powerful tractors, among others.

The main channels through which these new techniques and their use are introduced is the system of rural credits implemented by the dictatorship – still in force today – and the technical assistance sponsored by the state.

The way in which technical assistance is given to the farmers was copied from the North-American system, and the first agronomists who started to work under this system were paid directly by the Rockefeller Foundation and the Ford Foundation, under the excuse that they were giving assistance to poor countries.

The introduction of these techniques provokes several problems:

First, they are not adequate to the country's realities. They come from the USA and Europe, where the climate, the characteristics of the soil and the organization of agricultural property are completely different from Brazil's.

Second, they come together with a campaign to discredit the traditional practices of our peasants, and promote the use of chemical fertilizers, insecticides, poisons and machinery in general, as the only path agriculture must follow.

Third, they reduce research in experimental stations of the government to a mere test for the products and inputs produced by the multinational corporations. There is no research to answer the needs of the small farmers. In the past, research for Brazil's agricultural technology was carried out by Embrapa (58), a public concern that put its discoveries in the farmers' hands. Today this concern is bankrupt and technologies are controlled by the huge companies that impose their models for development. (59)

Fourth, they are linked to the use of toxics for agriculture, inputs that are already forbidden in their countries of origin because they seriously endanger the health of the farmers and the consumers of this kind of agricultural product. They have not only led human beings to their death, they have also seriously harmed nature, soil preservation, and the climate itself.

Because of this situation, these experts are already preparing alternative technologies that will be socially acceptable, economically possible, environmentally sustainable, and culturally adequate.

They come from the traditional practices of farmers and the scientific knowledge of our agronomists, and they are for the benefit of development and the well-being of society, and not just to make money for a few entities. (61)

The MST wants its settlements to use these alternative technologies, so it can be an example for small farmers in general. There are local initiatives to exchange information in the different regions.

Some concrete ecological actions

Diversify agriculture
The MST is determined to put an end to monoculture and to diversify agriculture, trying to guarantee a variety of products with sufficient quantity and quality for nourishment.

Preserve soil and fertilize it with natural products
It wants to combine crops, introduce others more adequate for our climate and our soil, and recover old varieties.

It must also use local power resources, making a rational use – not an indiscriminate one – of machinery according to the environment.

Production of ecological seeds

In some of the MST settlements they produce seeds, agricultural inputs and food under the guidance of ecology for agriculture. They are also recovering varieties used in the past and more adequate for each region, but discarded by the hybrid seed industry. In this aspect, the experience of the São Miguel D'Oeste, Santa Catarina, settlers and small farmers is outstanding, they have recovered nine varieties of corn and they are on their way to being self-sufficient in seeds. The settlers even produce organic or ecological seeds (with no poison or chemical fertilizers) for vegetables, and this is the basis for a totally organic and natural production of fruits and vegetables.

These seeds are sold under the trade name *Bionatur* by one of the MST cooperatives, called the Regional Cooperative of Settled Farmers/Rio Grande do Sul.

Another action in favor of ecology is the creation of nurseries for the production of seedlings, native trees, fruit trees and sometimes, even exotic species, within the settlements themselves.

Experiments with natural products to fight plagues

They are also experimenting with natural products to fight insects and the diseases that usually attack plants. Instead of using traditional toxic products, they are using natural practices, such as the fungicide known as *calda bordalesa* (62), biological control and natural insecticides.

Recently the MST approved 10 ethical commandments (63) that summarise their commitment with the land and with life, and are a guide for the consolidation of internal organization and the promotion of the well-being of the settlers.

First: Love and protect the land and nature's beings.

Second: Constantly improve knowledge about nature and agriculture.

Third: Produce food to do away with hunger among human beings. Avoid monoculture and the use of toxic products in agriculture.

Fourth: Preserve existing trees and replant new areas.

Fifth: Protect river sources, dams and lakes; fight against the privatisation of water.

Sixth: Adorn the settlements and communities, planting flowers, medicinal herbs, vegetables, trees etc.

Seventh: Treat garbage adequately and fight all practices leading to pollution and aggression against the environment.

Eighth: Practice solidarity and rebel against all injustice, aggression and exploitation practiced against any person, community or nature.

Ninth: Fight against latifundium so everyone can have a piece of land, bread, education and freedom.

Tenth: Never sell conquered land, for it is a legacy for future generations.

V – Diverse forms of cooperation

As we have already seen, since its foundation in 1984, the MST assigns a very important role to agricultural cooperation in its most diverse forms, in particular the most complete cooperation of all: cooperation in production, considered by the Movement as "the superior way to organize work." For a long time they believed that the Agricultural and Cattle-Raising Production Cooperatives (CPAs) were the most promising alternative for "socialization in the countryside and the formation of the new man." But when difficulties came up to reach the economic and social aims of production cooperatives, they understood that the best way to bring cooperation to the masses was to give priority to service cooperatives. Credit cooperatives were born later on.

They have created nine central cooperatives and 81 local ones for production, services and marketing, and three for credit: Crehnor, in Sarandi; Cooperados, in São Miguel D'Oeste; and Credtar, in Cantagalo. There are 45 more agro-industrial units.

Now we will analyze the lessons learned in all these years from the different experiences at cooperation.

COOPERATION IN PRODUCTION

Conditions

The MST learned that it could not force the implementation of cooperation in production; first it had to create the material and cultural conditions that would make cooperation among the settlers a possible and desired conclusion.

If during a meeting in a settlement you attempt to decree that they have to build a cooperative, no doubt this attempt will fail. It is the settlers themselves who have to decide how they want to work, and the situation will evolve from there.

Implementation of cooperation has to be very flexible and the forms adopted must take into account both objective and subjective conditions. (64)

Objective conditions

Among objective conditions, you must consider, in the first place, how much capital has been accumulated in the group that wants to start associating, and its possibilities of getting credit; in the second place, the kind of product they can produce; in the third place, the natural conditions of the environment; in the fourth place, the distance between storage centers – for example, you would not create a dairy in a settlement far away from the places where they will consume that milk. (65) But there is yet another very important factor: the technology you want to use, for if a peasant community still uses animal ploughs, the most logic thing is that it will work with the family; but if it has decided to use tractors and other machines for mechanized farming, the need to associate will become practically an essential thing to rent or purchase work instruments, even if that won't be the case for collective production, because the productive process itself doesn't require it. Things are different when a community wants to create an agro-industry to process pigs, for example; in that case collective work becomes a technical necessity:

a group of people will slaughter the animal; another will skin it; another will cut the meat; another will prepare sausages; yet another will pack them etc.

Subjective conditions

Of all subjective conditions, an important role is played by previous work experiences: workers on salary who have already gone through different forms of work division are better prepared for collective work than small peasants, used to work on an individual basis.

The political awareness of the families is also important, as well as their participation in the struggle for the conquest of land. The situation is very different for those who conquered their land through struggle, and that of peasants who have acquired it through an intermediary, like an adviser, a political party, churches etc. (67)

Varied forms

As we have already seen, cooperation in production can adopt very different forms, from the simplest ones, as is the case of mutual assistance, (68) in which the neighbors program their common activity so all of them will be able to participate, to the more complex forms of cooperatives for agro-industrial production, and the direct barter of services, in which payments or benefits have no role to play.

Common work (69)

Let us look closely at the different activities the workers of a settlement can carry out together, and still not have necessarily a process for collective production.

1st. Clean up the plantations: with "groups for mutual assistance."

2nd. Work and sow the soil with machines or oxen owned in a collective way; later on everyone cares for his own lot and tries to harvest it by himself.

3rd. Purchase machines, tractors and harvesters between all of them, so they work on individual lots.

4th. Build sheds to protect seeds, fertilizer and crops.

5th. Ask for bank loans with only one contract.

6th. Sell production at better prices.

7th. Purchase merchandise and inputs at the cheapest prices.

These are the main forms. There are numerous other kinds, like using a couple of oxen or a truck in common work. When the group carries out these activities but also does common work sharing productive tasks, then we have a group for collective work.

Each settlement, each community, each peasant must analyze with his comrades and freely decide what to do in a collective way. No one can be forced since, in the long run, the results are negative.

Advantages of cooperated work

Even if the MST insists that the peasant must not be submitted to pressure to join in a specific work method, the Movement encourages these forms of collective work of the land because it is convinced that, besides its individual advantages, it is "the only way to start changing society and arrive some day at socialism in Brazilian agriculture." (70)

Economic advantages

There are many advantages from an economic point of view. (71)

In the first place, it expedites access to credits, and this allows them to make more important investments in new technologies, such as storage, means of transportation etc. (72), because they are stronger to overcome banking difficulties The manager has a different attitude towards the person who already has a 100 million loan, than the one who only has a 10 million loan.

In the second place, work becomes more efficient and productive: there is an increase in agricultural productivity as a result of the concentration of a larger number of people that allows for a division of work.

It is interesting to point out that in spite of all the difficulties the MST cooperatives have had since the beginning, they are producing more than the average per hectare of the regions they are settled in. "There is a classic example: in Bagé, Rio Grande do Sul, a region of abandoned and unexploited latifundia, the settlements occupy about 5% of the municipality area and are responsible for more than 50% of its agricultural production." (73)

This increase in productivity is due to different reasons:

a) When several families unite and increase cultivated land, they can purchase means of production, like tractors and other machines with a higher technical quality, so they are more efficient; an isolated farmer will not buy a tractor, either because he doesn't have enough land to justify its use, or because he has no money and no bank to finance him.

b) Since the land is worked in a collective way, they can sow in the best season.

c) They take better advantage of the land, technically organizing sowing in small furrows that will avoid erosion and the crumbling of land as a result of heavy rains, respecting mountain areas, the worst areas, those for collective pasture etc.

d) Since the common area grows, they can sow different crops for market, like soy, beans, corn, rice. With individual work the trend is to plant just one market crop in the largest area, and the rest for their own on use.

e) There can be a better division of the kind of services each one will contribute to the group, according to his own specialization or preference. In the case of individual lots each farmer must do everything, so the results are inferior and the work lower in quality.

f) It makes getting technical assistance from agronomists easier. For these agronomists it is much easier to take care of a field of 1000 hectares with 100 families, than visit 100 families on ten hectares each.

g) It saves time on transactions in the city, so the peasant has more time for agricultural work.

In the third place, they can improve their infrastructure: electricity, drinking water, roads and other improvements, like building sheds, something nobody would be able to do on his own.

In the fourth place, they can purchase and sell at more convenient prices. If you buy 100 bags of fertilizer you get a better price than if you buy only 10, and if you sell 100 bags of wheat you earn more than if you sell only 10.

In the fifth place, they can face adversities under better conditions. When a temporary plague attacks their crops, or there are droughts or floods, the damage puts each individual farmer on the brink of bankruptcy, but in this case they can share the problem between all of them and it is easier to bear. When there is a disease in the family, the group keeps on working the crops and nothing is lost.

Finally, a very important thing: the MST settlements tend to activate the economy of the region, generating development, increasing trade and together with it, an increase in taxes. (74)

Social advantages

Cooperation also carries significant advantages from the social point of view.

First, it makes organizing society easier.

Second, it contributes to the solution of problems related to health, education, embellishment of the settlements, handiwork etc.

Third, if the families keep working together, they break down the social isolation existing on individual lots; the people get used to living in a community and improving their mutual relations.

Fourth, with the creation of kindergartens and collective dining rooms, it is much easier for women to join collective work.

Fifth, children who live in a community are brought up in a sounder environment and start learning in practice the importance of collective work.

Sixth, there are facilities for the families to have more time for recreation and develop cultural activities.

Seventh, there are no social differences because a peasant is doing better than another. All families make equal progress and face the same difficulties together.

Eighth, conditions are created to develop an attitude of help and camaraderie within the group, thus eliminating little by little each one's individualism and lack of solidarity.

Ninth, the fights that always take place in the neighborhoods are solved in a more democratic, healthier way, not like on individual lots, where things usually end in violence and the presence of the police.

Political advantages

From the political point of view, agricultural cooperation also has its own important advantages:

First, it creates a larger space for political discussion within the group, paves the way for understanding how society works, and makes for an increase in the social awareness of the people.

Second, they can form and then liberate cadres for the organization, and this in turn allows them to help other settlements and other struggles for the land without affecting agricultural work. In a study carried out by Concrab you can see how in five cooperatives with 154 families they liberated 18 militants full time and four others, part time. (77)

Third, they are stronger to defend the land against the governments, the large landowners or the bank and they are more convinced in their struggle for a broad agrarian reform and for deep changes in society.

Fourth, the peasants analyze their problems collectively, and the decisions made are the result of these analysis.

Fifth, it is an example and a point of reference for all small peasants, as well as for other sectors of society, since it proves that it is possible to organize economy, production and the life of the people, with a logic different from capitalism's.

Analysis of cooperatives for production

We cannot deny that there have been successful experiences for cooperation in production in the MST settlements, but that has not been the case in the majority of cooperatives because it is not an easy task to be successful in the creation of an alternative cooperative style, since it must penetrate the only existing market – the capitalist market, which, among other things, determines the lowering of prices of agricultural products while those for infrastructure and inputs increase.

But on top of these objective difficulties, the MST also made mistakes in production. Let us now study some of them.

Monoculture for the market

One of the Movement's major self-criticisms is that it went all out for monoculture for the market. That was a mistake, believes Stedile. The settlements should have produced not just for the market but also for their own use, thus keeping production diversified so as not to depend so much on the market or on price fluctuations. To produce only soy, or corn, or cotton, or yucca, is a huge risk. (78)

When they depend on the production of very few products, the peasants become much too vulnerable to the fluctuations of the market. On the other hand, monoculture imposes a cycle, particularly in the South, that leaves people unemployed for specific periods of time throughout the year. (79)

Exaggerated mechanization

One of the mistakes made in many settlements is the implementation – according to Stedile – of an exaggerated mechanization, not adjusted to the scale of production. If you have an area of 30 hectares, why do you buy a tractor that will be profit-making only if you have 100? (80) With such production possibilities, the money invested in the tractor will never be recovered to pay the debt they incurred in to purchase it.

It was largely due to the facility with which we were assigned credits between 1994 and 1996 that they encouraged the development of an agro-industrial structure, declares Álvaro de la Torre, but not the agro-industrial process as a whole. In a word, they started with a quite modern technical infrastructure that didn't correspond to the needs of production or to the training the people had to use this new technology. (81)

Today, the majority of the cooperatives are in debt and – what is even worse – the people have become very dependent on the State. In the past this wasn't true because the people counted more on their own power. The situation is more serious because during Fernando Henrique Cardoso's second term they decided to do everything possible to weaken the MST, ignoring all its demands.

We must explain, however, that the critical reaction to an exaggerated mechanization was not to refuse any kind of mechanization. No one in the Movement adopts that position – on the contrary, a certain degree of mechanization is necessary to help the peasant in his work and liberate part of the workers for other activities, wherever possible. (82)

If they use the tractor in rice plantations, they must organize themselves better to work in the garden; or in dairy cattle, or other activities that use labor force to yield higher incomes than when they used to work part-time. Nobody has said they will leave the tractor and go back to oxen. Oxen are useful only when the area is not suitable for a tractor. (83)

TRADE COOPERATIVES

Since the government has never had an agricultural policy that would take marketing into account (processing the products; transportation and roads to move production) the small farmer has only two ways out: "He either sells his production as cheap raw materials for the huge agro-industries, or he sells it retail to a population with no purchasing power." (84) Today, of every *real* earmarked for agriculture, 18 cents are for seeds, fertilizers and other inputs; and 70 for those who process and trade the products. The farmer keeps only 12 cents.

Coanol's experience

To face this situation we decided to create in Rio Grande do Sul a regional trade cooperative, Coanol, inspired in the experience of the settlements of the *Fazenda* Anoni, in which 370 families participate.

Coanol, which unites not only different settlements but also the small farmers of the region, collects the products of the partners, then processes them (cleans, dries and selects them), and takes them over to their respective industries. So it is not the peasants themselves who have to go through unscrupulous middle-men, but the cooperative that assumes this role and carries it out in a more professional way, with much more convenient prices: instead of charging 15%, like classic cooperatives do, they only charge 8% – practically the cost of transportation and taxes.

This has had collateral effects. The other intermediary concerns have been forced to lower their prices. And since the cooperative now works with many more products, it is much better prepared to negotiate with the concerns.

One of the main problems faced by trade cooperatives was market competition, because in this activity there are a lot of dirty tricks and even cases of corruption, like bribing the district attorney responsible for federal income so he will not charge the Tax for Merchandise Circulation, which is 17%. Or bribing the officer who classifies the quality of products, so he will classify them as having a higher quality than they really have, to be able to sell them at a better price.

MST cooperatives were able to see that some of their neighbors brought to market products inferior to theirs, yet were paid better. The explanation was this system of corruption we have just described.

The same thing happens when they have to purchase products.

Service cooperatives

Regional trade cooperatives later become service cooperatives. Both settled families and small farmers from the municipality or the region can become members. Even the CPAs. (86) There is no limit to the number of partners, which is not the case in cooperatives for production, which cannot have more than 30.

These cooperatives – that, as we said, became very common between 1995 and 2000 – organize the process of marketing production, inputs and consumer goods. They also give technical assistance and training and do some kind of planning at the municipal and micro-regional levels. (88) In the majority of cases they also process agricultural and cattle-raising products: they make pulping machines, microcenters for milk pasteurisation, cold-storage plants, rice harvesters, storage plants, and other things.

As we have seen, the settlements then start participating in the local or micro-regional markets. These cooperatives become points of reference for the settlers and for many small farmers of the region. Local trade, political authorities and local societies start looking at this experience with great respect. This growing prestige allows the MST to have a positive influence on the organization of other workers, not just the rural ones, but also the city ones. (89)

Even though the services rendered by these cooperatives have been very useful to their members, to be able to work efficiently and fulfill all the administrative requirements, they have had to look for trained cadres to take over these tasks, and they have been mostly MST cadres. When they go on to administrative tasks, they have to abandon their previous political responsibilities, and this weakens this aspect of the Movement.

CREDIT COOPERATIVES

In 1996, after organizing several cooperatives for production and regional service cooperatives, the MST started a debate on the multiplication of credit cooperatives. The idea was to use the settlers' savings, and become a unit that would pass state credits on to the settlers: like the Credit Program for Agrarian Reform (Procera) we have already mentioned.

At that time it was decided to follow up the Credit Cooperative (Credtar) constituted in Cantagalo, Paraná. It also started discussions in Sarandi, Rio Grande do Sul, to create another one (Crehnor). (90)

The Crehnor case in Sarandi

Let us see what happened in Novo Sarandi. (91) As we have already said, they had a trade cooperative: Coanol. With the capital it represented, it looked for credits in federal financial institutions, like the Banco do Brasil, Bndes (92) and the Bank of the State of Rio Grande do Sul (Banrisul), with the idea of passing them on to the small farmers and the settlers. These banks are interested in lending money to a credit cooperative because all the services the bank should give its clients are taken over by the cooperative.

The members of this credit cooperative must be organized groups or movements like the MST, the Movement of Small Farmers (MPA) etc. The cooperative assumes the drafting of the projects and the contracts and takes care of their registration. The farmer no longer has to go to the city, stand in line at the bank, lose time to get his financing; the credit cooperative goes to the community and puts a branch office there for this kind of activity. Among other things, it charges a very low interest rate for its services, only 7%, when the banks charge between 10 and 11%. On the other hand, it has thought about the possibility of creating a special credit line to help those who have difficulties. If the bank charges 1,4%, the cooperative would charge only 1%.

This cooperative started in 1996 with 34 members, but very quickly it began to grow and today it has more than 4600 members. That year, as a result of the struggles of the Movement of Small Farmers, they had created a special line of credit with a subsidy for them: the National Program for the Consolidation of Family Agriculture (Pronaf), but no bank was willing to assign it. The Novo Sarandi Cooperative took on this task. When the banks realized the success the Cooperative was having, they started trying to win over once again all those who had been excluded.

At the moment the Cooperative is present in 21 municipalities, and it does not cover more because it has not been authorized by the Banco Central. Since it received constant requests to extend its services to other municipalities, it asked this Bank for the authorization to increase this cooperative's area of action, but the bank preferred for other banks to assume that task, not the cooperative. Today it is common for people from the cooperative to find in their communities personnel from the Banco de Brasil and other banks talking with people: they have had to adopt the cooperative's way of working.

Crehnor has huge credibility because it works with organized movements and therefore, it has no delinquency rate. It always recovers the money it lends. If a member does not respond, it is the cooperative that assumes the responsibility. It does not assign individual credits, only if the person is a member of a group and has their solidary backing. This makes it easier to include those who have been excluded, because even if a farmer has very few resources, if he does have collective backing he will be assigned a credit according to his possibilities of assuming the loan – even if it is a small one, it is always something. (93) This makes the banks feel safe, they know that all the money they lend comes back.

Should we go to ward our own credit system?

They have come to the idea that the MST should have its own

credit system. Of course it would always have to sign agreements with other financial institutions, like the Chamber for Compensation, the Banco do Brasil, Bndes and Banrisul; services, though, would be organized in a cooperative, which would set the rules of the game.

Obstacles

But as always happens with any alternative to the existing capitalist system, the dominating classes cannot stand passively and accept this popular step in the field of credits. Recently, they started putting up obstacles. If in the past a cooperative could go into debt for 20 times the amount of its social capital, now it can do it only five times the capital. If in the past one could create a cooperative with 1000 *reais* (20 members with 50 *reais* each) now they require 50 000. On top of all this they are saying that credit cooperatives must be linked to a credit center, which must have eight times the net holdings of the cooperatives: 400 000 *reais*.

Debt and bureaucratism

But there is not only an enemy strategy to complicate things; there are also problems that come from the growth of the initial project of the MST itself.

According to Álvaro de la Torre, the original idea had been to create credit cooperatives whose size would be in proportion to the savings capacity of the member farmers. At the same time they thought those bodies would be able to pass on to the peasants the credits assigned by the state. The problem is that Crehnor grew too much, it has about seven or eight branches and since it is a middle institution for credits it must carry out a whole series of administrative and accounting operations that were previously carried out by the banks.

It has had to create such a huge administrative department that the members can no longer control it; even the chairman himself has difficulties unless he applies a very strict control. For example, he must make a daily balance of the activities, and this takes up a large amount of time. The members' control is done indirectly through a representative.

And since the savings of its members are not the only basis for its operations, it also takes care of transferring government credits, it ends up making a difference between the client who pays on time and the one who does not, and it tends to assign credits not to those who need them most, but to those who pay on time. And this is not all: since it must answer before the state for the reassigned credits, it has been forced to place debtors in the hands of justice.

The same thing happened with the service cooperative Coanol. Its funds went well beyond the savings capacity of its members.

De la Torre believes the cooperatives' capital should be only the sum of the quotas contributed by its members – the only way it could guarantee the payment of debts, and the members could feel they owned them. But this does not happen. Both the patrimony of credit cooperatives as that of service cooperatives comes mainly from sources outside the cooperative, and this is making the system collapse: the cooperatives are increasingly indebted, the members who leave the cooperatives don't pay their debts, and the technological package imposed makes them spend more than necessary on inputs, so their benefits are way down, and the problem increases.

Mário Schons, responsible for the credit cooperative Credtar, confesses that the situation is more difficult because – among other things – credit cooperatives are ruled by the laws of the Banco Central and if the Banco were to audit overnight, it would be in its right to do so. "If the cooperative wants to keep supporting the peasants, it has to recover the money it has lent, but if it uses legal power to recover the money, this will make the settler a landless person once again. That is the contradiction capitalism leads you to. To avoid this kind of problem, the cooperative itself takes measures: it analyses the monetary soundness of the peasant, and it assigns him only the amount of money corresponding to this capacity, even if he asks for more." (94)

Finally, over this long road the MST has been able to prove that existing laws are equivalent to a straitjacket over any attempt at creating a cooperative different from traditional ones. That is why it insists that the existing Law of Cooperatives be changed, and a law drafted to encourage the organization of workers' cooperatives different from traditional ones.

NOTES

1. "A settlement is made up of a group of families that work in an area of land for landless peasants, and they use it for agricultural and cattle-raising production [...]." J. P. Stedile and Frei Sérgio, *La lucha por la tierra en el Brasil*, Committee for Support to the MST in Barcelona (undated), p. 46. Original in Portuguese, Salvador, 1999.

2. Roseli Salete Caldart, *Pedagogia do Movimento Sem Terra*, Editora Vozes, Petrópolis, Rio de Janeiro, 2000, p. 120.

3. Op. cit., p. 121.

4. Ibidem.

5. We must remember that to get results from pressure for land, the MST tries to organize the largest possible number of landless peasants in a region to occupy an area.

6. National Institute for Colonization and Agrarian Reform.

7. See Chapter II: Occupy and Camp.

8. One of the advantages of the Bank for the Land is that the large landowners pay with money, not titles.

9. There used to be a law valid only for the state of São Paulo, which covered all public land within the territory of agrarian reform settlements. "With the 1982 elections, which brought about a political change in the state government, a new setting was created for the agrarian situation in the state of São Paulo. José Gomes da Silva occupied the Department of Agriculture and implemented a project

to regulate the estates." B. Mançano Fernandes, *A Formação do MST no Brasil,* Editora Vozes, Petrópolis, 2000, p. 67.

10. This *fazenda* is in the south-eastern part of the state of São Paulo. It covers 17 500 hectares and the two municipalities of Itapeva and Itaberá. These lands that used to belong to the state had been rented by the government to large tenants, who wanted to get hold of Pirituba through legal measures. B. Mançano Fernandes, *A Formação do...,* op. cit., p. 67. But the land was mostly abandoned.

11. *Jagunços.*

12. Pirituba is 30 kilometers from the frontier with the state of Paraná. I came from a region 100 kilometers away.

13. Pastoral Commission for the Land.

14. This word is used in Brazil for the agricultural settlements where the houses are grouped in only one place.

15. Beans.

16. For practical reasons we talk about the Pirituba (name of the old *fazenda)* settlement, but at present there are six settlements there created from 1986 on, when the MST started to occupy these lands and conquer part of the *fazenda.* Sometimes, instead of speaking about six settlements we talk about "areas," "but in practice they are settlements created on the same *fazenda* during the last ten years." Norberto Martínez, notes to this work, December 2, 2001.

17. He is referring as an analogy to the period Cuba has gone through after the defeat of socialism in Eastern Europe and the USSR.

18. She speaks about "nuclei at the base," but to avoid confusion with "nuclei of militants," we have decided to use the term suggested by J. Pedro Stedile: "group of families."

19. The MST tends to consider opportunists the peasants who are assigned land without having gone through a previous process of struggle.

20. It no longer exists. It was eliminated in the year 2000 by the Fernando Henrique Cardoso Administration.

21. She is referring to second grade in primary school.

22. It is equivalent to fourth grade in primary school.

23. It is equivalent to secondary school.

24. See the development of this aspect in Chapter IV: Education.
25. This is how the MST calls their kindergartens.
26. Workers Party.
27. In Brazilian Portuguese: *pelego.*
28. Party of the Brazilian Democratic Movement.
29. J. P. Stedile and Frei Sérgio, *La lucha por la tierra...,* op. cit., p. 47.
30. Ibidem.
31. MST, *Construindo o Caminho,* Movimento dos Trabalhadores Rurais Sem Terra, São Paulo, June 1986, p. 164.
32. Norberto Martínez, notes to this work, August 2, 2001.
33. MST-Concrab, *O que levar em conta para a organização do assentamento,* Caderno de Cooperação Agrícola N° 10, May 2001, p. 12.
34. Ibidem.
35. These conclusions have been developed in depth in the brochure *O que levar em conta...* op. cit., pp. 12-14.
36. The defect of this circular distribution is that it is not very flexible. It is based on the belief that the number of settled families will be stable for a long time, but that is not the case.
37. Parishes are always built as a result of the settlers' initiative.
38. J. P. Stedile, notes to this work, July 31, 2001.
39. MST-Concrab, *O que levar em conta...,* op. cit., p. 9.
40. Álvaro de la Torre, interview by Marta Harnecker, op. cit.
41. Norberto Martínez, Notes to this work, November 5, 2001.
42. Sort of licence given by the government to use the land while the final title is assigned.
43. Letter that backs the peasant so the bank will authorize a credit.
44. MST-Concrab, *O que levar em conta...,* op. cit., p. 14.
45. Ibidem.
46. Op. cit., pp. 14-15.
47. Op. cit., p. 19.
48. On the characteristics of this school, see the chapter of this book on this subject.
49. Information given by Vilanice Oliveira Silva, member of the MST's national coordination in Ceará and national coordinator of the health sector, interview by Natalia Alvarez, Havana, April 13, 2001.

50. Every religion can be used to either alienate or free man.
51. Gilmar Mauro, Article "*O MST e o Meio Ambiente*", *Nação Brasil* magazine, N° 122, September 2000, pp. 22-25.
52. Ibidem.
53. During colonial times, black slaves, forced to live a miserable life in areas around their owners' *fazendas,* fled in large groups toward the mountains, organizing areas where they lived in freedom; the were called *quilombos.* The largest of them all, on the frontier between the states of Alagoas and Pernambuco, came to be known as *República dos Palmares* (1618-1698). Ganza Zumba and Zumbi were its main leaders. Some historians have calculated that 30 000 blacks lived on these *quilombos.*
54. On this subject, see MST-Concrab, *O que levar em conta...*, op. cit., pp. 15-17.
55. Op. cit., p. 16.
56. Op. cit., p. 17.
57. Ibidem.
58. Empresa Brasileira de Pesquisas Agropecuárias.
59. J. P. Stedile, *"Terra de todos",* interview in the magazine *Caros Amigos*, June 2000, p. 32.
60. MST, *Construindo...*, op. cit., pp. 200-201.
61. Op. cit., p. 201.
62. Mixture of copper sulfate and lime with water.
63. Taken from the magazine *Sem Fronteira*, December 2000, N° 285, p. 21
64. J. P. Stedile and B. Mançano Fernandes, *Brava...*, op. cit., p. 117, Braz. Ed., p. 101.
65. Ibidem.
66. In Brazil, municipal representatives are called *vereadores.*
67. J. P. Stedile and B. Mançano Fernandes, *Brava...*, op. cit., p. 118, Braz. Ed., p. 102.
68. In Brazilian Portuguese: *mutirão.*
69. Taken from *Construindo o caminho*, MST, São Paulo, 1986, pp. 186-187.
70. Op. cit., p. 190.

71. Op. cit., pp. 191-192.
72. J. P. Stedile and Frei Sérgio, *La lucha por la tierra...* op. cit., p. 50.
73. Op. cit., p. 48. Stedile recognizes, however, that in the beginning "many people were against the division of labor because they mistook division of labor with capitalism." At that time they didn't understand that this division – a natural result of the development of productive forces – could be used not only to exploit people but also to improve living conditions in general. A brochure published by Conrab explains that when division of labor was first studied, they did not take into account the alienation produced by the Taylor model; see Concrab, *A evolução da concepção de...*, op. cit., p. 17.
74. J. P. Stedile and Frei Sérgio, *La lucha por la tierra...,* op. cit., p. 48.
75. *Construindo...*, op. cit., pp. 193-194.
76. Op. cit., pp. 192-193.
77. Concrab, *A evolução da concepção de...*, op. cit., p. 26.
78. J. P. Stedile, interview by Marta Harnecker, May 22, 2001.
79. Op. cit.
80. Ibidem.
81. Álvaro de la Torre, interview by Marta Harnecker, Porto Alegre, May 13, 2001.
82. J. P. Stedile, interview by Marta Harnecker, op. cit.
83. Op. cit.
84. Elena Ferreira, quoted by Otto Figueiras, *"Sabor de Campo"*, *Sem Terra* magazine, Year III, N° 10, Jan-Feb. 2000, p. 37. Op cit., p. 37.
85. Vilmar Martins Silva, leader of the Novo Sarandi Agricultural Cooperative, Rio Grande do Sul, interview by Marta Harnecker, September 1999.
86. Concrab, 1997, pp. 62-71, quoted by B. Mançano Fernandes, *A formação do MST...*, op. cit., p. 233.
87. Vilmar Martins da Silva, interview by Marta Harnecker, op. cit.
88. B. Mançano Fernandes, *A formação do MST...*, op. cit., p. 233.
89. Op. cit., Concrab, *A evolução da concepção de...*, op. cit., p. 23.
90. Concrab, *Sistema...*, op. cit., p. 34.
91. Waldemar de Oliveira, leader of the Credit Cooperative Crehnor, interview by Marta Harnecker, September 1999.

92. Bndes finances investments only, while the Banco do Brasil finances investments and operational expenses for agricultural production.
93. Here ends what Waldemar de Oliveira explained in the interview already mentioned. On the other hand, according to Norberto Martínez, assigned credits are related to annual production and not to long-range investments – they turned out to be very difficult to control
94. Mário Schons, interview by Marta Harnecker, Santa Catarina, May 2001.

CHAPTER FOUR

EDUCATION WITHIN THE MST

I – First experiences

At first, the MST's main priority was the struggle for the land, but even then it was concerned with education.

Proof of this are two experiences in Rio Grande do Sul: Encruzilhada Natalino – one of the MST pioneer camps – and Anoni, from which they learned many lessons.

Encruzilhada natalino

After Encruzilhada Natalino was occupied in 1981, the families put up their black canvas tents and started living in the camp, building their organization little by little.

A swarm of children – around 200 – ran around and played in the camp area. They spent their days at their parents' meetings and assemblies, mile-long marches, hunger and confusion.

Aware of the children's anxious state of mind, some adults

started thinking about what to do with them. There were groups of mothers who guided the children's games, explained why they were camping, and even made them join some of the camp's activities. At that time nobody thought about the possibility of a school; their main concern was how to care for those children and avoid their being too much in danger because they lived on the roadside. They also knew they had to analyze with the children the struggle in which "they were forced to participate." (1)

Little by little, the children understood why their parents were fighting and they too began to defend the idea.

Chance would have it that among the campers there was a teacher – Maria Salete Campigotto – who later became the first teacher of a settlement. She took over the coordination of the childrens' activities.

A year later, part of the families from Encruzilhada went to other lands that had already been earmarked for the peasants. There were 180 school-age children, 112 of whom did not know how to read or write. That situation began worrying the parents.

At that time Maria and another teacher, Lúcia, started to encourage the fight among the campers to create a first-to-fourth-grade state school in Nova Ronda Alta (ex Encruzilhada Natalino, in the Ronda Alta Municipality). After many talks and meetings, the Department of Education authorized its construction. That was in 1982, but the school became legal only two years later.

Inspired by the ideas of the great pedagogue Paulo Freire, these pioneer teachers started promoting systematic meetings with the parents and launched the first experience of a "different" school for landless kids. This school had to teach the students how to read and write through their own life experiences, enhancing "the history of the struggles of these families and their love for the land and for work." (2)

ANONI

Another interesting experience took place in Sarandi. In 1985 landless farmers occupied the *Fazenda* Anoni, creating the biggest camp so far: 1500 families and more than 2500 children gathered there.

To assume the different tasks, they organized work teams, including the education team made up of people interested in working with the children. According to the protagonists, in the beginning no one thought about a school, nor did anyone talk about it. Like in Encruzilhada, the challenge was to explain to the children why they were there and organize them in groups to sing, run and play.

But months went by, no solution appeared for the campers, the people in the education team started thinking about a school within the camp itself. The team was divided in two: those who didn't agree because they believed the school could affect the larger battle they were waging, it could be an obstacle for the mobility and the active participation of the families in the struggle; and those who thought land would not be assigned in a long time and if the need to educate the children was not assumed, many parents would decide to leave the camp. And since there was also the possibility that Anoni might become a settlement, the school would not be so provisional.

People who were there at that time recall the difficulties behind the internal negotiation to get support from all the families for the battle to be waged for an official school in the camp.

The first thing they did was find out how many possible students they had. There were 650 children between 7 and 14 years old. Then they looked for experienced teachers. They discovered that there were 15, and there were also several people who had not completed first grade but wanted to help. This information was decisive to convince the undecided parents on the need to organize a school within the camp.

The education team started training in Popular Education and made contact with the teachers Maria and Lúcia from Nova Ronda Alta.

At the same time they created a parent-teacher commission to negotiate with local authorities. The commission had its first meeting with the Sarandi mayor, and was able to get him enthused with the idea of creating a school within the camp; but in the second meeting, the mayor said "it would be difficult to get government approval because the school was for a camp – in other words, a not yet legal area of conflict." (3) Later on, in 1986, thanks to the contact of a teacher from Porto Alegre who knew the Secretary for Education, a meeting was arranged with him, but once again there were only promises but no solutions. Time went by and still the children had no school.

The following year, they decided to go to the mayor's office once again; there they found several pieces of plastic canvas to make a huge tent where they would put all the schoolrooms, and that's where they started their lessons. They had three shifts: 23 teachers for 600 students between first and fourth grade.

After a time the state approved the building for the school. It was the first official school in an MST camp. When the schoolyear was over they moved to the new school.

In 1987, shortly after the school had been built, some significant events took place in the camp. There was an operation to expel them: a huge police siege was organized around the *fazenda*, forcing the landless peasants to go out to Cruz Alta (municipality in the central region of Rio Grande do Sul). As a reaction to this siege there were important manifestations throughout the state.

"The teachers talked to the children and their parents and decided to participate with them in all these events. One of the teachers went on the famous pilgrimage made up of 30 children, who left Anoni and crossed the state requesting support for the struggle for agrarian reform." (4)

This combination of what was going on in the camp and what happened in the classroom had positive results: little by little, parents, teachers and children began to change their opinion and understanding of the educational process. They started believing they should fight for a different kind of education, centered on the campers' reality. People wanted their children to understand everything that was going on around them and to participate in this action to transform it.

Later on, while the occupants were being settled, Anoni was divided into 16 areas: the families occupied a whole *fazenda* made up of 9000 hectares, so now it was impossible for all the children to go to the same school. Then they started struggling for more schools and, thanks to that struggle, they were authorized seven state schools for the camp. This "confirmed the strength of the organization and called attention on the school question in all MST groups within the State." (5)

As you can see in these two examples, the path followed by landless peasants to make the state assign schools for their children is quite similar to the one they go through to get land to settle. Negotiations can take months and even years, so both campers and settlers are forced to begin with improvised schools.

We must point out that in the case of the settlements – already recognized legally – the state has the legal responsibility to create schools and guarantee conditions for their activities.

ORIGIN OF THE TEACHERS

This unity between the school and the camp would have been impossible if the teachers had not camped with their students.

The truth is that in the beginning the teachers were all camped, and the municipality signed a contract with them for a specific amount of time, as an emergency measure, since their curriculum was insufficient. They had no degree, so they could not be candidates for a public bidding to the post.

In 1988, the Department of Education did not renew their contract, and substituted them for a group of state teachers who knew practically nothing of the campers' life. "What they did know [...] was that they were being sent to a place it was very difficult to get to, with precarious work conditions, with 'eccentric' people who called themselves landless people – and all that for a miserly salary." (6)

The experience was a total flop. When it rained, there were no classes because those teachers weren't able to get there; and when there were classes it was difficult to convince the children – who perceived the difference between a teacher from the camp and another from outside – that what they were learning with the new teacher could be important and attractive.

So the MST understood the need to have graduated teachers in the camps and the settlements, "because this would help in the negotiation of contracts with the state" (7) and thus avoid that outside teachers be imposed.

On the other hand, they also understood that this opposition between teachers "from inside" and those "from outside" couldn't be absolute. "The point wasn't to exclude all those teachers who did not live in the camp, but to demand that each teacher – no matter where he came from – be really engaged with the children and the community." (8)

A SCHOOL LINKED TO OUR LIFE

That first school in Anoni was a different kind of school. According to professor Neive, it was an "essentially practical" school that taught "aspects that could influence the work and the organization of a new life"; it was an instrument that made the struggle go forward, without that absurd separation between what was going on in the settlement and what they studied in the classroom (9); but most especially, it was a school that taught its students that "reality is something you can change." (10)

As opposed to traditional schools, where the teachers receive their teaching program all made up by the Department of Education and all they have to do is apply its contents, in our settlement the parents and teachers agreed on what should be taught their children: they had to be taught concrete things, like why people had camped and with what horizon in mind.

It was important to start out from reality, but at the same time teach the children other new and unknown things, because they could not be limited only to MST experiences. They have to be prepared for life with a global and critical vision of the reality they live in.

You can teach them Portuguese, math etc. Starting from the concrete experiences of their life, adapting the program you receive all nice and pat but completely foreign to the experience of the students.

It is as essential to discuss what you are going to teach as it is how you are going to do it.

The methodology and the very relationship teacher-student has been a huge challenge, particularly for the teachers with previous experience in this field: "They had to abandon the traditional way of working: people were used to teach traditional education, come to the schoolroom and just talk", emptying the contents of their teaching materials into the heads of the students, as though they were empty containers.

"In a camp things are different. The children question the people, they are more open, they are better prepared to ask the teacher." (11) "The teacher is no longer the lady who commands but the comrade in struggle, who knows and who teaches, but who also listens and learns. And the children – who are so sensitive to the new experiences they are observing or living together with their parents' struggle – are the great teachers of this different school." (12)

If the teacher comes from the same place, the relatioship becomes easier, but if he comes from outside the camp he must first start by breaking down "the traditional concept – particularly in small rural communities – where they see the teacher as the top authority, the absolute ruler of school knowledge." (13)

The following anecdote is a good example of how you can form children in democratic behavior. One day, the "Landless Kids" (14) decided to organize an assembly with all the students of the school. They elected the child who was going to chair it and decided on the agenda. This called people's attention because it meant the children were beginning to feel responsible for things. During the assembly the students analyzed the snack the mayor had promised them a long time before – there they decided to go to the municipality and speak with him, demanding he keep his promise. (15)

In settlements where work is organized in a collective way, often the children feel motivated to create their own organization. In Nova Ronda Alta, for example, the children got used to holding weekly assemblies to analyze their daily problems and distribute the tasks they could take on in the settlement. These experiences make it easy for the school to be a miniature organization of the sectors and work teams in the camps and the settlements.

II – PROPOSAL FOR A DIFFERENT SCHOOL

A SCHOOL TO PREPARE THE "NEW MAN"

The "different" school proposed by the MST is radically opposed to the "official" traditional school, which, on top of being an instrument to reproduce the ideology and the customs of the ruling classes, is a powerful tool of the capitalist system to prepare cheap labor for its industries: it does not educate people, it prepares "parts" of a productive machine, all they have to know is what is absolutely necessary to carry out their work efficiently, they must not have their own opinions, nor think with their own brain – they must do their work "automatically." So they create human beings who are not only individualistic, competitive and machista, but also passive and dependent.

On the contrary, the MST schools concentrate their work on the integral preparation of the children, on the preparation of "a new man and a new woman, for a new society and a new world." (16)

For this integral preparation of people who have suffered so much oppression and discrimination, the MST uses professor Paulo Freire's teaching methods, printed in what he called *Pedagogia do Oprimido* (17) together with José Martí's (18) and Anton Makarenko's. (19)

The MST does not cater to the theory of a specific teacher or current; rather, it incorporates elements from many academicians. It is this confrontation with practice that makes specific ideas become incorporated and others discarded. There is no doubt that this permanent relationship between theory and practice, and the corroboration of what is written through action, is the direct consequence of the "fact that the people are part of a social movement", (20) which is constantly making, unmaking and remaking its stand.

"MST pedagogy is, therefore, the result of the implementation of different teaching methods that history has accumulated." The Movement adapts and modifies them according to each specific context. The point is to prepare a "teaching method answering people's needs in their settlements and within the MST." (21)

A NEW KIND OF PEDAGOGY

The idea is to form men and women able to actively assume the evolution of their own future – to become agents for social transformation.

This teaching method does not take people as though they were empty bottles to be filled: it is based on the idea that it is not only the teacher who knows, but that each person has his own specific knowledge and all these different knowledges have to be shared so everyone can walk the educational path together. It believes the students don't start off from zero in this process, because "they bring with them an enormous accumulated knowledge, a very rich history that must be enhanced." (22)

This new kind of pedagogy wants to form human beings who will be the protagonists of their own learning process, builders of their understanding of the world. People ready to learn from each other, enrich each other in their constant search.

A school with these aims in mind cannot be guided by "a closed teaching model, be it the most 'revolutionary' in the world, by a specific teaching method, a static organizational structure" (23) – rather, it must be open, using a teaching method where everyone really has something to learn and something to teach, always, all the time. (24) Just like life: it follows the rhythm of mankind and its protagonists, the people.

The MST teaching method is made up of different elements that constitute its main body (25): social struggle (the "contradictions, confrontations, victories and defeats"); collective organization (the organizational experiences of the camp or settlement); the land (that has a deep meaning for the peasant); work and production (education for work and through work); culture (both the life style generated by the MST and the way landless people are and live, their mystique, their symbols for the struggle, religion, art etc.); the power of election (people are educated when they have the possibility of voting – individually or collectively – and think about their elections); history (train memory and understand the "live" contents of history: something built by people); and the balance between school and community. (26)

MAIN PRINCIPLES OF THE EDUCATIONAL STAND OF THE MST

The educational stand of the MST is based on the following principles:

First: educate taking reality as a starting point. "School must teach how to read, write, and analyze reality – both local and general – and teach through practice." (27)

Second: teacher and student are comrades who work together, learning and teaching each other: there are no teachers who know everything, nor students who must receive this knowledge passively.

Third: education must prepare the student for manual and intellectual work. (28)

Fourth: it must recover and encourage values such as solidarity, comradeship, collective work, responsibility, love for people's causes.

Fifth: "it must asssume the person's integral development." (29) The main aim, as we said, is to form "a new man and a new woman, for a new society and a new world." (30)

Sixth: school organization (31) must create the conditions necessary for the children and young people to develop in every direction.

TEACHING PRINCIPLES

The following are the teaching principles guiding this new school:

Study and work

Convinced that work is an essential value and that a child comes to love it only if he also learns about it in school (32), the MST believes that at school, children must not only study but also work. The child must learn all kinds of things, and he must learn by doing them, while learning at the same time the social importance of work. (33)

Self-organization

School cannot be just a place to study and work; there, the children will also learn how to organize themselves. They must be active participants of the school's tasks and organization: group work; decision-making; planning and analyzing the activities carried out by all the students and teachers, among other things. (34)

Democratic participation (35)

At school they also learn about democracy, implemented through the daily relationship among the students, the students with their teachers, the teachers among themselves, and the school with the settlement. They learn to make decisions, respect others, respect decisions made by the whole group, and put these decisions into practice.

School: part of the settlement or the camp

It is important that children's work and organization within the school be related to life in the community, and for the latter to follow the school's development, assuming it as part of the settlement or the camp. At the same time, the whole community "and not just the parents of the students, must analyze the school's guidelines", (36) because this victory belongs to all the families.

An MST school is not based on a curriculum full of information; but on the experience lived by the children: at work, organization, new forms of relating to each other, questions that come up along the way, new discoveries, daily problems of the community.

Characteristics of the teachers

"MST schools can't have just any kind of teacher." (37) They must be with the children during work, help them organize themselves, guide them. They must not make all decisions, but rather stimulate the children to do so. At the same time, they must participate in the life of the settlement. A purely technical training is not enough, they must also have political training.

Integral education

An MST school must form not only the children's minds. It is important for them to learn how to care for their bodies and their health; to "cultivate and express their feelings and discover the full sense of life in all its manifestations; they must learn to fight and be firm in the struggle, but never lose their tenderness or sensitivy, and always be angered by injustices." (38)

ORGANIC STRUCTURE OF THE SCHOOL

After having observed "that the way the school functions is also a formative and educational experience", the MST believes that "to make a school different it is not enough to change the curriculum and alter methodology in the classroom. *The way in which the school is organized* and the *social relations* thus generated are as important as the contents and the methods." (39)

That is why since 1994 the educational sector has been drafting a proposal for this new kind of elementary school be. (40) This proposal has undergone several changes and improvements provoked by the errors and successes the MST schools have lived through their practical work.

This methodological proposal includes the organization of both students and teachers at school and in the community, working and supporting them.

Students

It is suggested that the students organize themselves according to groups of activities. Just as in the camp or the settlement their parents must participate in groups of families, so in the school, the basic organization are these groups of activities. The students "must be challenged to organize themselves", electing their coordinating representatives, their substitutes and the schoolroom's secretaries.

These groups can study together what they have learned in the classroom; do their homework; help clean and embellish their classroom; distribute snacks; prepare the mystique etc.

Another way the students can organize themselves is in *classrooms groups* to promote: assemblies, draft regulations for the life they share in the classroom, analyze the educational process, propose voluntary work, debate the school's guidelines etc.

Another suggestion to organize their work is for the students to form *work brigades*, mixing the members from different groups of activities as well as from different schoolrooms.

A good example of this self-organization is the experience of the student cooperative, which began in 1989 at the *Construindo o Caminho* [Building the Road] School, in the Conquista da Fronteira settlement, Santa Catarina State.

To improve the relationship between theory and practice, they thought of organizing the school like a cooperative, since this is something the children know well. The idea was for them "to be able to understand the organization of the settlement and contribute to it." (41)

At the beginning of the school year, the teachers talked with the students about the main activities they would be carrying out in school, and for them to do this in an organized way it was essential to create work teams. There were four of them: cleaning, general services, survival, and teaching and communication. The children themselves chose the names of each group, its work contents, as well as the coordinators (who constitute a deliberative council) and the secretaries. Each student chose the group he wanted to work in.

It was also necessary to draft internal rules, which the children discussed with the community. When someone goes against these rules he is judged by the whole school, "and if necessary, also by the settlement's commission for education." (42)

Kindergarten children are also part of the cooperative-school and participate in practical activities according to their own possibilities (they distribute pencils, help clean up, water the plants, organize their games etc.).

196

When organizing major activities where they have to negotiate – for example, teaching materials, adult work, transportation – the work teams define what they need and start negotiating with the leaders of the adults' cooperative.

Another case of self-organization took place when "a school principal attacked the students. She called them stupid, marginal kids, tramps, and the students organized themselves and threw her out from her post. It was something that started with the students themselves." The vice-principal had participated in a recreational activity of the MST, and since this principal didn't like the Movement she had dismissed her. So the students "rebelled so much with what was going on that all together, they drafted a letter, got more than 500 signatures to endorse it, and then sent it to the delegation. They were able not only to get the vice-principal back into the school, but they threw the principal out and the vice-principal took over." (43)

Educators

Besides being able to participate in the camp's or settlement's groups of families, within the school itself the educators (44) can organize themselves in a *teachers' collective*. There they can analyze the educationalcand teaching process, plan the year's activities etc.

Community

It is very important, at the same time, for the community to contribute "to the school's teaching process through the MST leaders and sectors: they must follow the work carried out in the school and participate in seminars or plenary meetings where they can study, analyze and set the guidelines for the teaching-learning process and the political and pedagogical proposal." (45)

One of the ways for their participation as a *settled or camped community* is to create volunteer teams to improve the school; pass on to the children and the youth the history of their struggles; control their sports and teaching activities; help out in the classroom or substitute for the teachers when they are off to training courses, for example. They can also follow the steps taken by the school, and analyze its needs.

School instances

The school must create spaces for the participation of all the educational elements, which include:

The Assembly – the main instance – which must convene the students, educators and the community once or twice a year to elect or ratify the members of the Student Council and elect its leaders; adopt the political-pedagogical project for the school, the curriculum and the internal rules and regulations.

The Student Council, made up of representatives from the students and the community, the educators, and the education group. Its mandate can last one or two years. The meetings can take place on a monthly basis to contribute to school management, study the educators' work, organize activities, for example.

This instance can call joint plenary sessions or meetings of students only, or the community only, according to the subject to be discussed.

School leaders, elected by the students, the teachers and the community, "can become a school coordination, opening up space for the participation of students' representatives." (46) So they apply collective leadership and share their tasks and their power with the other members of the coordination.

Management instruments

Internal rules and regulations

"It is very important for the school to draft its internal rules and regulations with everyone's participation, defining the rules of behavior for both educators and students." (47) Basically, they are rules for their life in common, so they can be changed whenever they want to.

These rules found at an MST school can be a good example of this: "Create rather than adapt; have fun rather than compete (particularly in physical education); keep your school clean; respect others when they speak [...]; try to be friendly with everybody: avoid fights." (48)

Participative planning

Another good idea for the school to work well is participative planning, "to guarantee an integration of the different levels of school life." (49) This can be done at different instances: state and regional collectives for education (where the guidelines received from the education team can be adjusted according to the demands of the camp or settlement); and at school, to draft the yearly, weekly or individual classroom plan.

Collective evaluation

Collective analysis is another basic instrument for the educational process. It must be constant, participative and democratic and include both students and professors with the community. Since it is designed to overcome problems and improve the work of those involved, it must stimulate the correction of errors, rather than just imposing sanctions.

The experiences we have described so far are from South Brazil, where the MST's educational process is more developed. But reality is very different in other regions.

In the South, they have very important accomplishments in different fields, like opening MST schools in settlements – sometimes with teachers who militate in the Movement, while in others the Sector for Education controls the teachers imposed by the state – in other regions, children must go to official schools and the MST uses extra-curricular activities to apply its own educational policy.

In the Northeast, where illiteracy rates are very high, there are interesting experiences to teach young people and adults to read and write. (50)

This process has not been void of difficulties, progress and adversities. One of the things to be improved is the still-existing gap between the theory of the MST project for education, and its practical implementation in the classrooms.

III – THE MST, THE MOST IMPORTANT SCHOOL FOR LANDLESS PEOPLE

Even if school has an essential role to play in children's education, the Movement and its struggle constitute the most important school of all. (51)

Today they already talk about "MST pedagogy," to refer to the way the Movement has been forming (52) its people for the past 17 years of struggle. As a place for the education of Brazilian landless people, the MST teaches its members in day-to-day life and the peasants say: "The Movement is our most important school." (54)

Permanent struggle: strategy for education

The MST has learned that "everything is achieved fighting, and that fighting educates people." One can understand why keeping landless people "in a permanent struggle is one of the most striking pedagogical strategies the Movement has come up with." (55)

"Contradictions, confrontations, victories and defeats" (56) generated in the struggle itself mean a huge lesson. If you think about the struggles, analyze their results, see what went right and what went wrong, you will accumulate knowledge and develop a better capacity for analysis.

The MST believes that the learning method must go from practice to theory, and back again to practice; this means that only if you participate in the struggle while analyzing reality will you be able to develop a critical stand and increase your awareness. As Paulo Freire said: "Nobody educates anybody, nobody educates himself, people educate themselves mutually, through their collective organization." (57)

Life in the community

On the other hand, by relating its members with others, both individually and collectively, unlike they did in the past: sharing everything with everyone, working in a cooperated way, fighting for collective improvements rather than individual ones, "things start changing in their heads and hearts, they recover values that had been lost or ignored." (58)

"I learned as a mother, as a woman, as a teacher – says teacher Salete Campigotto. As a mother: a different way of bringing up my children. As a teacher: I came from traditional teaching and inside me there was a revolution, a confrontation with the kind of education I had learned. When I started working with my students on what they had gone through in Encruzilhada Natalino and Nova Ronda Alta, I came up with the idea of a different kind of school. I also learned to overcome many barriers as far as gender discrimination is concerned; I discovered the importance of women in the struggle for land. For me, the MST was the most important university I could have attended." (59)

Taking root in a collective group

Finally, thanks to its participation in the organization and in the struggle, the MST is able to create among its members a political and cultural identity, as they start "recovering roots, recreating relations and traditions, cultivating their values, inventing and remaking symbols representing new social relationships" (60), that appear throughout the struggle.

IV – INSTANCES, SEMINARS AND COURSES

FIRST NATIONAL SEMINAR

MST's educational position has evolved over a long period of time. Already in July 1987 it held the First National Seminar on Education, with representatives of commissions for education (61) from six states. Two things came to light: how would they build the schools? and what was pursued through them? These aspects were the starting point for the pedagogic proposal centered on "the reality of landless families." (62)

Similar events were carried out in different states to articulate existing actions to create a sector for education. At that time the MST "started defining political guidelines for education in its schools." (63) And it set itself the goal of "learning the truth about education in the camps and settlements; guarantee together with state and municipal governments the right of all children to school, as well as their activities; develop a proposal for education centered on the realities of a transforming community; integrate the schools and the teachers in the organization of the settlements and the camps; stimulate relations with educators and institutions in order to prepare training courses for the teachers; invest in literacy programs for young people and adults." (64)

SECTOR FOR EDUCATION

In 1988, after an internal reorganization that divided work in the Movement according to sectors of activity, they created the Sector for Education.

At that time its main task was to organize the struggle for public schools – first to fourth grades – in the settlements, and in some places also in the camps. The other task was to "have available men and women teachers meet with representatives of the communities, where they could start analyzing the development" (65) of a project for a "different kind of school", which two pioneer women teachers from Nova Ronda Alta, Rio Grande do Sul, had already started defining.

On the other hand, with the creation of the Sector for Education, the first steps were taken to overcome the challenges related to illiteracy and poor schooling.

One of the investigations carried out between 1994 and 1995 in camps and settlements linked to the MST, showed a 29% illiteracy rate among these people. But in some far-away places in the North and Northeastern regions, the figure was much higher. On one hand, some people aren't registered as illiterate because they know the different letters and how to write their name, but they have huge difficulties in interpreting texts and working with numbers – they are really semi-illiterate. This is one of the enormous problems for the MST and its educational efforts.

As far as schooling for children is concerned, the investigation showed that only 1.6% finished elementary school; and about 20% of the children and 70% of the youth and adults had no school for them. (66)

Wanting to overcome this, the MST also launched a series of activities involving different institutions, and by the mid-90s "it was able to increase the number of literacy courses for young people and adults in the settlements and camps, organizing training courses for the teachers at the same time." (67)

NATIONAL COLLECTIVE FOR EDUCATION

From 1989 and 1994, the MST was hit by the government's strong political repression against social movements in general, and started an "intensive work for education and internal organization." (68) It is precisely at that time – one of the most fruitful as far as "organizational progress and pedagogic thinking" is concerned – that they created the National Collective for Education, "responsible for a more articulated and intensive work in each state," (69) and they began to take over more rigorously the graduation of teachers for MST schools. This is how educators' training became a priority.

COURSE FOR TEACHERS (1990)

"Another aspect that came to light in the 90s was the concern for the quality of education: the need to prepare a teaching method, a proposal for education, that could merge the requirements of the sector and the political project of the Movement – says Edgar Kolling (70). One of the elements that allowed the Movement to go forward as far as quality was concerned, was the creation of a teachers' course. First it included the teachers from Rio Grande do Sul, later on all of the Southern Region and finally, the whole country. It was like a lab course, where they made pedagogic analyses (school-time) as well as practical experiments (community-time), because during vacation in January, February and July, the teachers attend this course, and in March-June and August-December, they stay in the communities and give classes." (71)

Besides aiming at an adequate training for the teachers according to the educational challenges, they wanted to give them teacher's diplomas so MST educators could access to teaching posts in state schools. (72)

TECHNICAL COURSE (1990)

At the beginning of the 90s they also created – as we have already mentioned in another chapter – the Technical Course for Cooperative Management (TAC) to prepare technical personnel. Both this course and the teaching one had students from all of Brazil.

Iterra (1995)

Because of the importance these courses started accumulating, in 1995 it was decided to create the Technical Institute for Training and Research in Agrarian Reform (Iterra), in Veranópolis, Rio Grande do Sul. Its aim is to organize educational and research activities answering the MST's needs. Though the main emphasis is placed on organizational and technical training, the rest of the educational aspects are not overlooked. (73)

A year after its foundation, the Josué de Castro School was created within Iterra, where they teach primary and secondary school for those who have been unable to attend regularly; a Teachers' Course and a Course for Technicians in Settlement Administration, whose first students graduated in 2001. In 1996 they also organized a Course for Health Technicians.

Joining theor y to practice

Adhering to the MST proposal for education, these students – whose average age goes from 17 to 25 years old – learn by joining theory to practice: while they study, they help manage the institute and carry out practical activities in their communities. Because of this and because they aim at the integral training of people (74), Iterra is organized in different "times": (75)

School-time

The students stay at the institute for about 75 days. They divide their time between what is called class-room-time (seminars and training workshops, where they study theorical aspects) and work-time (three hours a day in the bakery, the kitchen, the laundry, the garden, or the industrialization and marketing of agricultural products). In this way they contribute to the school's self-reliance. "The institute is managed by the students themselves." (76)

Community-time

Another 75 days are devoted to the practical stage; the students return to their camps or settlements and there, besides working with their community and participating in their struggles, they must read books and do practical work for their different courses at school. (77)

A school similar to life

Iterra "is a school where study does not come before work, rather the students try to reproduce life there as it really is [...], with its challenges, problems and solutions." (78) For example, if you have children, you take them with you; they are not an obstacle for you to study there. This is positive because "the children bring to the school the atmosphere of a family. Those who feel nostalgic and would like to embrace a son can do so by embracing someone else's son. These children are mostly taken care of as a collective group. And if someone gets sick, everybody takes care of him."

This is how the MST "tries to create conditions for people to be aware that life goes on. It goes on because they have to work, take care of their children, make coffee at breakfast and lunch, be responsible for the school's independence. It is attended by women and men, particularly young people, from the whole country", so there is an enriching cultural exchange: "there are people from the Northeast, black people, Polish, German, Italian descendants etc. This mixture allows someone from the South to have a better idea of what the Northeast is all about, and the same goes for someone from the Northeast, who gets to understand much better what is going on in the South. The MST tries to make the maximum use of this fusion of regions: it stimulates integration and tries to avoid regionalism, without destroying the rich patrimony each person carries with them from their place of origin." (79)

Florestan Fernandes National School

Wanting to develop social and political training and "intensify studies and research on the reality they are building", the MST is creating the Florestan Fernandes National School, in the Guararema Municipality, São Paulo. The courses last for two and a half months of intensive study; they are designed for militants still in training. They get basic knowledge on the MST and its history; political history of Brazil; history of the struggle for the land; history of revolutions; struggles in Latin America; introduction to philosophy, economy and sociology. (81)

Agreements with universities

Recently, the MST has become concerned with the university training of its members, and it is promoting agreements with different universities.

For example, "during 1998-99, Concrab (82) signed an agreement with Iterra and the universities of Vale do Rio dos Sinos (Unisinos) in San Leopoldo; Rio Grande do Sul, and with the University of Brasília (UNB), to create a course for Specialization and Extension of Cooperative Administration, in order to graduate settlers and technicians from the Cooperative System of Settlers (SCA)." (83) At present this course is given by agreement with the University of Brasília, the State University of Campinas (Unicamp) SP and Iterra. There are also teaching courses for the teachers, by agreement with the University of Unijuí (Rio Grande do Sul), the Federal University at Paraiba, the Federal Unuiversity of Espírito Santo, the State University of Mato Grosso, the Federal University of Pará, the Federal University of Juiz de Fora, and the State University of Rio de Janeiro (UERJ). (84)

On the other hand, around 45 young people from the MST from

different regions of Brazil are being trained as doctors in the Latin-American School of Medical Sciences in Havana, Cuba.

MEETINGS AND CONFERENCES

First Enera

To open the debate on education in the countryside, in 1997, the MST organized the First National Meeting of Men and Women Educators for Agrarian Reform (Enera) in Brasília. Around 700 teachers from settlements and camps from 19 states and the Distrito Federal; literacy specialists and child educators met to expose and debate their own experiences. The best part of the meeting was the presentation of the "Manifest of Men and Women Educators for Agrarian Reform to the Brazilian People" (85) – a political synthesis of the MST proposal for education.

Another important aspect of this event was the proposal to create the National Program for Education in Agrarian Reform (Pronera), implemented in 1998 by agreement between the MST and Incra and several universities. This initiative, however, has not been fully developed, in particular because of lack of resources.

The federal government signed an agreement through Incra that opened the door for teacher training and the development of literacy programs for young people and adults. But there have been difficulties from the very beginning: on one hand, the government wants to impose its own proposal for education, and goes into a permanent conflict with the MST over this; on the other, they never give the necessary resources, there is always too little money for the activities and to pay the teachers. (86)

First National Meeting for Men and Women Educators of Young People and Adults was held in 1998, in Recife.

National conference for basic education in the countryside

Also in 1998 was organised by the MST the National Conference for Basic Education in the Countryside, organized by the MST, the National Conference of Brazilian Bishops (CNBB), the University of Brasília, Unesco and Unicef. There, they analyzed the experiences in different regions of the country, and debated public policies and teaching projects to carry this proposal of Basic Education in the Countryside forward.

Itinerant school for camps

On the other hand, since MST camps are not necessarily installed in those areas that will later be assigned to the occupants, or that often the families are thrown out by the police, the need came up for a school that would adapt to this unstable situation. So in 1996 they created the Itinerant School in Rio Grande do Sul, with the approval of the State Council for Education, which recognizes the validity of the studies for those who attend them. "This school goes wherever the camp goes in its struggle for the land." (87)

It admits students from first to fifth grade, classes are given by camp teachers, others who are part of the group of Itinerant Schools, and MST militants, the majority of whom have been trained in the Teachers' Course in Iterra.

Kindergartens

Stable cirandas

From 1996 on, the MST has called its kindergartens *cirandas* because this word implies playing, while the traditional name *creche* refers to what is formal and obligatory.

Children's *Cirandas* are stable educational spaces for children from 0 to 6 years old who live on MST settlements. There they play and learn elementary things, as well as "singing, drawing, playing, writing, and acting, all according to their age." (89)

The creation of these *cirandas* reflects an evolution within the

MST, which now considers children as its own patrimony, seeds for future transformation and struggle. The Movement has understood that the responsibility to educate and train children does not fall only on the parents – and particularly the mothers – but also on the Movement asa whole. (90)

It is also important to explain that the *cirandas* are organized only when several women in the camp or settlement are already incorporated in production, and the community feels that a *ciranda* is a concrete necessity. "You must first go through an analysis with the families for them to understand the importance of a *ciranda*." (91) This requires a joint effort by the community to get the material resources and the teachers or people willing to become educators.

In some cases, the infrastructure necessary for the *cirandas* has been partially financed by Unicef, but most of the time it has been financed by the settlements themselves.

"A large part of the methodology for teaching is still being thought out and the people are trying" to put it into practice little by little. (92)

Itinerant cirandas

Itinerant Children's *Cirandas* work during events organized by the different MST sectors. It is "a parallel structure to allow people – in particular landless women – to participate in courses, seminars and congresses held outside settlements and camps." (93) The creation of this kind of *ciranda* had been claimed by women collective groups, known from 1998 as gender collective groups. (94)

MST bibliographic materials

From 1991 to 2000 the MST has published 25 documents on education, including 11 booklets (methodology; primary, youth and adult literacy programs; school planning; games; principles; basic education etc.); 6 bulletins (school in the settlement; mystique; communication; work and cooperation; development of education in Cuba…); 8 booklets of the collection Making History and Making School; as well as 11 additional documents specifically for children.

V – LIMITATIONS AND DIFFICULTIES

Schools with limited material conditions

"One of the important limitations we still have today is that in general our schools have very poor material conditions: no libraries, deficient teaching equipment and resources," says Edgar Kolling. (95)

Educators: quantitative and qualitative deficiencies

Another limitation "that is still a serious problem" is the insufficient training of the teachers. From about 6000 educators in the settlements, more than 3000 have no specific training for the work they carry out; there are people in teaching roles who have finished only primary school. (96) The biggest challenge is to improve the training of teachers both from a qualitative and a quantitative point of view" (97), since in the end, the still low number of people working in the Movement's educational sphere is an obstacle for organization in this sector. (98)

Even if in several places the MST has been able to have elementary education (up to eighth grade) in the settlement itself, this does not mean it is directly in charge of the MST educators. Most of the time the teachers have signed a contract directly with the state, and because of the already-mentioned selective methods used, it is difficult for MST militants to be accepted.

We must make a huge effort to "win" "outside" teachers over to our cause, so they will feel empathy with the ideas of the MST. (99) There has been "a long struggle with teachers who were completely against the aims of the Movement." (100)

This situation implies the Education Department must organize work outside the school with the teachers, the parents and the "Landless kids." To teach the children the history of the Movement and its principles, they must use extra time after school, saturdays and sundays, and this is no easy thing. "The educators who are not academically graduated teachers work with the children in different ways: through games, study activities and educational workshops. They also work with teenagers – among other things, to create values." (101)

Spaces for discussion and analysis must also be created with parents and teachers on the Movement's proposal for education, which is very different from "the official ready-made school, where the teachers don't worry about their community. [...] Books, for example, come all ready and packaged for the schoolrooms, and this we interpret as alienation, because people don't learn to question themselves and their own environment. Our books, on the contrary, are made in such a way that the educator has to prepare his work plan – how to plan and what to plan for – according to the situation in each different settlement." (102)

The São Paulo government, on the other hand, eliminated the secondary schools that already existed in the rural communities of the region – and they were quite numerous – arguing that it had to cut expenses in rural education, that education was better in the cities, and that the peasants would benefit from this new system. But obviously this policy goes against the MST proposal for education, which is based on the premise that "if people are farmers, they must develop their practical activities in the country from a very early age, because that is the best way to learn: they can see plants come out and grow, they can see animals, production, how their parents work. The Movement believes this training directly related to life, is basic for the cultural education of our peasants." (103)

No budget for these programs

Another example of the bureaucratic and political difficulties we have with the state is what happened with Pronera, the literacy program already mentioned, which was accepted by the federal government and implemented nationally. The program was first financed by the government and the MST was directly in charge of managing resources and preparing its proposal for education.

Unfortunately, right now it is very difficult to do this because of lack of resources. The MST puts the blame directly on the neo-liberal policy, which becomes evident in the way the government has cut Incra's budget. (104)

CONSOLIDATING ITS PROPOSAL FOR EDUCATION

The MST has gone a long way to guarantee the right of its people not only to quality rural education, but also to its own proposal for education in line with the aims of its struggle. In spite of the obstacles it has had to overcome – not so much for lack of resources as for the barriers put up by the government – the MST has won important battles, both from a quantitative and a qualitative point of view. It has consolidated its efforts to define a proposal for education – in a critical and participative way – for the formation of the new man. (105)

The emphasis placed by the MST on education is undoubtedly part of the solid base for its future development and gives it as a social movement, a much broader and all-embracing dimension.

NOTES

1.   Roseli Salete Caldart and Bernadete Schwaab, *A Educação das Crianças nos Acampamentos e Assentamentos*, in Frei Sérgio, J. Pedro Stedile, *Assentamentos...*, Editora Vozes, Petrópolis, Rio de Janeiro, 1991, p. 88.
2.   Ibidem.
3.   As told by Bernadete Schwaab, teacher at Anoni, in Frei Sérgio, J. P. Stedile, *Assentamentos...*, op. cit., p. 90.

4. Op. cit., p. 92.
5. Op. cit., p. 91.
6. Op. cit., p. 93.
7. Ibidem.
8. Ibidem.
9. Op. cit., p. 97.
10. As told by teacher Neive in F. Sérgio and J. P. Stedile, *Assentamentos...*, op. cit., p. 102.
11. Op. cit., pp. 99-100.
12. Ibidem.
13. Op. cit., p. 98.
14. The name "Landless Kids" was made up by the very children who participated in the First State Meeting of Landless Kids in São Paulo, in 1997. After that, the MST used this definition, which somehow reflects that the "Landless" identity starts at an early age.
15. Frei Sérgio and J. P. Stedile, *Assentamentos...*, op. cit., p. 100.
16. *O que queremos com as escolas dos assentamentos*, Caderno de Formação, N° 18, São Paulo, 1999, p. 3.
17. Paulo Freire wrote his main book, *Pedagogia do Oprimido*, in 1969, during his exile in the United States. From 1964 to 1965 he wrote *Educación como práctica de la libertad,* "first theoretical exercise on Brazilian literacy." Miguel Darcy de Oliveira, in *El proceso educativo según Paulo Freire y Enrique Pichón Riviere*, Ediciones Cinco, Buenos Aires, second edition, 1986, p. 42.
18. Cuban patriot, poet and writer.
19. Russian pedagogue.
20. Edgar Kolling, general coordinator for the National Collective of the Sector for Education, interview by Luis Acevedo Fals, Santa Catarina, Brazil, May 2001.
21. Op. cit.
22. Maria Salete Campigotto, interview by Luis Acevedo Fals, Ronda Alta, Brazil, May 2001.
23. Roseli Salete Caldart, *Pedagogia do Movimento Sem Terra*, Porto Alegre, 1999, document.

24. Ibidem. The MST proposes a school "that will not be a fixed model" or a "prescription for all times and places"; rather, it is a series of teaching principles "coming from the history of the Movement" and, therefore, not valid for all times, but able to transform themselves just like the dynamics for stuggle can be transformed too."

25. See more on this subject in: *MST, Como fazemos a escola de educação fundamental,* Caderno de Educação, N° 9, MST, Setor de Educação, Rio Grande do Sul, 1999, pp. 6-11 .

26. They call "school-time" the hours in which activities are carried out in the school itself, and "community-time" those for practical activities and the investigation of the students' reality, op. cit., pp. 10-11.

27. *O que queremos…*, op. cit., pp. 7-9.

28. Op. cit., p. 9.

29. Op. cit., p.11.

30. Op. cit., p. 3

31. This subject is developed further on in "School Organic Structure."

32. *Construindo o caminho…*, op. cit., p. 31.

33. *O que queremos…*, op. cit., pp. 12-13.

34. Op. cit. This idea is developed further on in "School Organic Structure."

35. Ibidem.

36. Op. cit., p. 16.

37. Op. cit., p. 19.

38. Op. cit., p. 20.

39. *MST, Como fazemos a escola de educação fundamental,* Caderno de Educação N° 9, Rio Grande do Sul, 1999, p. 3.

40. Elementary school goes from first to eighth grades.

41. *Construindo o caminho…*, op. cit., p. 31.

42. Op. cit., p. 32.

43. Marcia Mara Ramos, interview by Marta Harnecker, Pirituba Settlement, São Paulo, May 2001.

44. The MST has recently started to use the term "educator" instead of "teacher" to name "all those directly involved in the school's learning-teaching process." Educators are the teachers (settled or not); the officers engaged to work in the school; settled voluntary peasants,

and the technical personnel who contribute to the settlement and its educational process. (*Como fazemos a escola...*, op. cit., p. 17).

45. Ibidem.
46. Op. cit., p. 20.
47. Ibidem.
48. Op. cit., pp. 20-21.
49. Op. cit., p. 21.
50. Marcia Ramos, interview by Marta Harnecker, op. cit.
51. *Como fazemos a escola...*, op. cit., p. 5.
52. See the difference between forming and educating. Forming implies a much broader process than education. So school is only part of "a broader experience for the human formation of this collective group."
53. Op. cit., p. 24.
54. Quoted in several texts by R. Salete Caldart, and in MST, Caderno de Educação, N° 9, *Como fazemos a escola...*, op. cit., p. 5.
55. R. S. Caldart, *Pedagogia do Movimento...*, op. cit., document.
56. Ibidem.
57. Christiane Campos, militant in the MST formation sector, interview by Marta Harnecker, Montreal, February 22, 2001.
58. R. S. Caldart, *Pedagogia do Movimento...*, op. cit., document.
59. Maria Salete Campigotto, interview by Marta Harnecker, Ronda Alta, 2000.
60. R. Salete Caldart, *Pedagogia do Movimento...*, op. cit., document.
61. A first step was the creation of parent-teacher commissions "to demand and organize schools in camps and settlements." Bernardo Mançano Fernandes, *A Formação do MST no Brasil*, Editora Vozes, Petrópolis, Rio de Janeiro, 2000, p. 176.
62. Ibidem.
63. Ibidem.
64. Ibidem.
65. R. S. Caldart and Edgar Jorge Kolling, *O MST e a educação* in *A Reforma Agraria e a Luta...*, Editora Vozes, Petrópolis, 1997, pp. 228-229.
66. B. Mançano Fernandes, *A Formação do...*, op. cit., p. 223.
67. Op. cit., p. 224.

68. R. S. Caldart and E. J. Kolling, *A Reforma Agraria e a Luta...*, op. cit., p. 229.
69. Ibidem.
70. Edgar Kolling, interview by Luis Acevedo Fals, Santa Catarina, Brazil, May 2001.
71. Ibidem.
72. Frei Sérgio, *Assentamentos...*, op. cit., p. 104.
73. Salete Caldart in B. Mançano Fernandes, *A Formação do...*, op. cit., p. 224.
74. "We believe school formation must be integral, work and class-room, but it must also take into account social relations, political-ideological education, gender-related problems [...], we are very much concerned with the creation of sentiments [and values] in people, anger against injustice, giving your life for others," says Edgar Kolling.
75. Edgar Kolling, interview..., op. cit.
76. Ibidem.
77. Christiane Campos, interview..., op. cit.
78. Edgar Kolling, interview..., op. cit.
79. Ibidem.
80. In B. Mançano Fernandes, *A Formação do...*, op. cit., pp. 224-225.
81. Ivanette Tonin, interview by Marta Harnecker, November 16, 2001.
82. Concrab: Confederation of Cooperatives for Agrarian Reform in Brazil.
83. B. Mançano Fernandes, *A Formação do...*, op. cit., p. 245.
84. Christiane Campos, interview..., op. cit
85. Together with their demands for education, the educators declare their commitment to the struggle for agrarian reform and social transformations; they express that as part of the working class they must take a stand: anger against misery and injustice; education as the main axis of any process for social transformation; urgent need to put an end to illiteracy; need for pedagogic methods based on democratic participation and concerned with all dimensions of human beings. R. S. Caldart, *Pedagogia do...*, op. cit., pp. 265-266.
86. Christiane Campos, interview..., op. cit.
87. MST, *Balanço das atividades do setor de educação do MST*, July 2000, document for internal circulation.

88. In this case, the word *ciranda* refers to a Brazilian song and popular dance that goes: "*ciranda, cirandinha, vamos todos cirandar...,*" and refers to the game ring-around-the rosy.
89. *Revista Sem Terra*, Year II, N° 8, 1999, p. 38.
90. Christiane Campos, interview..., op. cit
91. Ibidem.
92. Ibidem.
93. Ibidem.
94. Christiane Campos, interview..., op. cit.
95. Edgar Kolling, interview..., op. cit.
96. In Brazil, this primary schooling is known as "fundamental" schooling.
97. Edgar Kolling, interview..., op. cit.
98. Taken from the article "*O movimento dos trabalhadores sem terra e a educação: a perspectiva da construção de um novo homem e de continuidade do movimento*", by Marcia Regina de Oliveira Andrade, *A Reforma Agraria e a Luta do MST*, Editora Vozes, Rio de Janeiro, 1997. p. 261.
99. Delwek Mateus, MST leader in the Pirituba Settlement, São Paulo, interview by Marta Harnecker, May 2001.
100. Marcia Mara Ramos, interview..., op. cit.
101. Ibidem.
102. Ibidem.
103. Delwek Mateus, interview..., op. cit.
104. National Institute for Colonization and Agrarian Reform.
105. The MST now has 1200 schools for basic education; 3800 educators for basic education; around 150 000 students; 1200 young and adult educators; 250 educators for kindergarten children. (Information taken from *Balanço das atividades do setor de educação do MST*, July 2000, document for internal circulation).

CHAPTER FIVE

INTERNAL ORGANIZATION

I – CHARACTERISTICS OF THE MST

A MOVEMENT OF LANDLESS PEASANTS

The Movement of Landless Rural Workers is a social movement emerging as a peasant movement of small farmers used to family work. (1) When it was institutionally founded during the 1984 First National Meeting, it didn't choose the name of "peasant movement" but that of "movement of rural workers", not for theoretical reasons but simply due to the fact that Brazilian peasants don't use this term to refer to themselves, they prefer to be known as farmers or rural workers, to which they add the term "landless" because the movement groups small farmers, either landless or with low-quality land where they can't survive with their families.

Categories of landless peasants

The category "landless" includes different kinds of small farmers: sharecroppers or partners (together with their family, they work on someone else's land with their own tools and sometimes even their seeds, while the owner contributes only the land and sometimes the seeds and the fertilizers; production is divided between the owner and the sharecropper, and when each gets half, then the peasant is called *meeiro*); tenants (they rent the land at a fixed price that does not depend on the size of the crop, and can be paid in cash or in kind); occupants (they settle down on someone else's lot – most of the time, unproductive land belonging to the State or an unknown owner – and work it as owners, even if they lack the property title (2)); rural day laborers (who sell their work to any landowner for a salary; you can find among them many tenants, partners and small owners who are forced to work for a salary at specific times of the year); small agricultural owners (who own a small lot – up to 5 hectares, depending on the region (3) – whose production is insufficient to feed their family, so they want to get more land); and finally, the sons of the small agricultural owners, who usually lose their peasant status when they form their own family and enter the landless category.

AIMS IT PURSUES

That the land be held only by those who work it

The MST fights so in Brazil, land will be held only by those who work it and live on it. It believes that if someone speculates with the land, uses it to exploit other people and does not cultivate it, he has no right to own it. Aware that in present-day capitalist society it is impossible to carry out a radical agrarian reform, it is fighting to build a new society and a new economic system.

A DIFFERENT PEASANT MOVEMENT

The MST is different from other classic peasant movements. Several of its traits set it apart:

It incorporates the whole family

The MST incorporates the whole family, both in the struggle and in decision-making; from old men to children, where women play an important role in everything they do – contrary to unions, for example, where only adult men participate. This participation on an equal footing makes each member of the family feel he is taken into account, and this strengthens both his decision to struggle and his commitment.

Women oppose the police just like their husbands and sons. You can see them very actively in the main places for social integration, like the school and the kindergarten, and very often they also participate in production. Slowly, women start to take over posts previously occupied exclusively by men. There is an increasing number of women in MST administrative tasks, coordinating productive sectors and political work at the top echelons. (4)

But it is young people who make up the main body of the Movement, unlike what usually happens with peasant movements or urban unions;, this one renews itself constantly as more young people come into its ranks. In general, the militants are between 16 and 30 years old.

Pluralist

At the same time, it is a pluralist popular movement, because it integrates landless rural workers, no matter what race, religion or party they belong to, as long as they respect the Movement's rules.

Made up not only of peasants

It includes everyone who wants to fight for agrarian reform. So the Movement is not made up exclusively of landless peasants. It also includes: the settled peasant – who already has his land, but is still in the struggle to make it produce – the agronomist, the technician in agriculture, the economist, the priest, the retired lawyer, and anyone willing to militate so Brazil can finally solve the problem of all landless peasants, contributing to a radical agrarian reform.

Even though the spinal column of the movement and the majority of its members are rural workers, having cadres who are not peasants – what we could call "organic intellectuals" of the MST – has helped it fight against cooperativism and learn from their experience, thus enlarging its vision of what aims it pursues on the medium and long run.

Though the qualitative weight of these organic intellectuals in the Movement is very important, the majority of the political leaders are rural workers.

Promotes mass struggle

While the MST was getting organized, its experiences in the struggle made it understand that social victories are conquered only as a result of mass struggle, with the massive participation of the people.

"If we are satisfied with having only a bureaucratic organization with no mobilization power; or if we cling to the governement waiting for our rights to be respected only because they are written down in a law, we will get nothing at all. Nothing – declares João Pedro Stedile. Rights established in the law are no guarantee whatsoever for popular victories. They are taken into account only when there is popular pressure. [...] The people will attain their victories only if they wage a mass struggle. That is what really changes the political correlation of forces in society. Otherwise, it is the status quo itself that will solve the existing problem. A social problem can be solved only through social struggle, it is part of the struggle of a class against another." (5)

Only if they fight will the peasants have the necessary strength to defeat latifundia and conquer the land; if they start to move instead of sit waiting for the government's "divine" assistance, or believing in a bunch of bureaucrats' measures.

The strength of the dominating classes resides in their economic power, the use of the law and the armed forces; the strength of the people resides in their capacity to unite, organize and mobilize themselves. That is why the MST mobilizes the masses whenever necessary.

You can almost assert, therefore, that the MST "would lose its main identity if it stopped being a social movement known for the organization of struggles and mobilizations involving an increasing number of people. The struggle for the land is waged directly by the landless peasants and not by their representatives. (6)

National mobilizations

Unlike the majority of other peasant movements that tend to organize their struggles at a local level, without taking into account their historical context, the causes behind their problems and the way society works as a whole, the MST understood it is essential for the struggle for agrarian reform to have a national scope – the only way in which it will represent a "confrontation with the general policies of the bourgeoisie and its project." (7)

Struggle agains the peasants individualistic culture

The majority of peasant movements defend only the immediate interests of this social class, strongly linked with the peasants' individualistic culture, who fight for personal property over the land and once this is achieved, they want to work it only with their family.

The MST, on the contrary, insists that its members overcome this individualistic culture, through deep changes aimed at cooperation and solidarity.

Not only a social, but a socio-political movement too

The landless movement is not limited to a social movement with sectorial interests alone; it has a general political scope, it is what some define as a socio-political movement. From the very beginning it understood it could not stop at the corporative stage. Thanks to previous experiences, it learned that in spite of being a social struggle based on peasants, the struggle for agrarian reform was headed toward failure if it stopped at the corporative stage; it could go forward only if it entered the global social struggle.

"If a family only fights for the land and loses its ties with a larger organization, the struggle for the land will have no future whatsoever. It is precisely that larger organization that will transform the struggle for the land into a struggle for agrarian reform [...], the superior stage of corporative struggle." And that is precisely where the "political ingredient" comes up. (8)

Though it has assumed this political ingredient and believed that it must participate as a movement in the country's political life, it has never foreseen the possibility of "becoming a political party" (9), understanding nonetheless that the existence of a political instrument is essential for the deep social transformation it pursues.

Trade-union corporative element in the MST

Even though the movement's characteristics are different from those of other peasant movements – usually centered exclusively on union or corporative interests – this doesn't mean the MST overlooks the demands in struggles or reduces the importance of the trade unions to attain these aims.

It not only organizes the struggle for the land – the main motivation to incorporate a peasant family – once this is achieved, it continues fighting, as we have seen, for other claims: credits for production, roads, public lights, schools, medical services, better prices for their products. This proves that "the MST does have a union corporative element" (10), because it also fights for specific demands and interests of the peasants.

On the other hand, what really contributes to establishing mutual trust among its members in a longer-range struggle is its efficiency in achieving more immediate economic objectives.

Relationship between the MST and the union movement

The relationship between the Movement of Landless Rural Workers and the union movement has changed according to circumstances, following the evolution of the latter.

The MST has never opposed the union movement, but it believes that all by itself it will be unable to solve the essential problem of transforming the limited struggle for a piece of land into a struggle for agrarian reform. That means that the trade unions are able to wage the battle for land, but it stops at the corporative level, so the peasants don't develop their awareness.

The MST is also very critical of the way in which the union movement organizes its base for corporative struggles.

But since the Movement is for the unity of all the workers, it has always tried to coordinate its struggles with those of the union movement.

Little by little, however, the MST has come to realize that it was very difficult to work within the trade-union structure.

"The government controlled the trade union to such an extent that you couldn't do much in that straight-jacket. We had to organize our base for this confrontation and try to identify other ways to struggle, because the existing unions improvised their own struggles and the government took advantage of this situation to keep them at bay: it changed the time for the meeting, so the day ended and no meeting was held, and the trade-union leaders had to go back empty-handed," says Frei Flávio.

"What proved once and for all that the union structure had reached its ceiling was the 1995-96 struggle against the drought, which had really affected the farmers. It's after that struggle, in 1996, that the Small Farmers' Movement – (MPA) was founded.

This movement started with prolonged struggles, one or more weeks-long, imitating the MST's. The peasants were mobilized for 2, 4, 10 days, until they got what they wanted. It did away with the idea that a farmer could not abandon his home for more than a day because of his chores: milking the cows, feeding the animals, among other things. To solve this problem the movement encouraged group organization: in a family of 10, two would be mobilized and the other eight would help out at home, so there were no problems for those two to be away for five or six days. The unions had never thought of something as simple as that." (11)

The MPA began to organize within the trade unions. In many municipalities, all union members are in the Movement; in others, the union is against it, but in spite of everything there is no confrontation. It has a legal personality as a civil association, organized in about eight states, in some better than in others. From day one it has been closely linked to the MST, which has supported and advised it.

Aware that the MST had conquered the Procera – favorable agricultural credit we have already mentioned – through the struggle, the MPA began working with MST assistance for a subsidized credit for small farmers. Though they finally got it, the government has not stopped creating contradictions between both movements: it put an end to Procera and now the settlers must fight for loans that come from the same fund as that for small owners. As Frei Flávio says, "the government reduced food and increased mouths." (12) To break this divisionist strategy, the MPA and the MST are trying to negotiate together. Survival is at stake.

Autonomous peasant movement

The MST is an autonomous and independent peasant movement, which follows its own internal rules and as far as its activity is concerned, is not submitted to any foreign authority. Though it is in good relations with the union movement, it does not depend on its leadership at all. It works with progressive sectors of numerous churches, in particular the Pastoral Commission for the Land of the Catholic Church, like the but it comes under no church jurisdiction whatsoever. And finally, though the majority of its members are either militants of the Workers' Party or vote for it, this doesn't mean this political party has any voice at all in its internal life. The MST does not come under nor does it depend on these bodies.

"We constitute an autonomous social movement, that uses its own head, walks on its own two feet and has fraternal relations with all the other organizations," declares João Pedro Stedile. (13)

And since this independence can be achieved only when there is financial independence, one of the tasks before the Movement is to find its own resources. (14)

II – Essential principles guiding the movement

Organize rural workers at the base
Convinced that only a strong and autonomous organization would be able to pursue the MST objectives, the founders of the Movement stressed the organization of landless rural workers at the base, with the family group as the main organizational cell.

The workers themselves must lead the movement
From the historical experience of other peasant movements, the MST has learned that it is possible to go forward and conquer agrarian reform only if the leadership of the movement belongs to the workers themselves. That is why it is essential for the Movement to prepare its leaders in all directions. (15)

Equal participation for women
The MST fights against machismo, so entrenched in the peasant

world. Women must receive facilities and encouragement to participate at all levels of action, power and representation. (16)

It believes any kind of gender discrimination must be eliminated in all of the movement's activities, and it must fight against machismo in all its facets that hinder working women's equal rights and conditions.

For this, women commissions must be organized in settlements and camps to discuss their specific problems.

Women's active participation must be encouraged in MST commissions and other bodies at the different instances: municipal, state, national; their articulation within the union movement must also be encouraged, coming together with the rest of rural women workers, without taking into account their category – unifying landless women workers, small women owners, salaried women workers etc.

At the national instance there is a Gender Collective that first started as a Women Collective. Their first responsibility was to think, propose and plan specific policies for the organization of landless women, and submit them to the National Leadership and Coordinating Committee. They understood later that the subject concerning women should not only be a feminine concern, rather it should be a concern for all of the MST – so they created the Gender Collective, made up of both men and women.

The struggle must start against machista culture, which impregnates the world of women, since the majority of them consider themselves only men's assistants. They must start to understand that they have a specific contribution to make to their collective group and to society as a whole.

The MST is convinced that equality between men and women will be achieved only if there are equal opportunities for both, and this is in direct relation with the training both sexes receive. That is why it has decided that in all training courses, half the students must be women. And as is well known, it is not enough to be a learned person to solve this problem, but one must also exercise responsibilities in day-to-day life, the MST also believes women must be present on an equal footing with men in the coordination of family groups and in regional coordinations. It is only in state and national headquarters where capacity is the ruling criterion for specific tasks. (17) That is why the important weight of women at this level is more significative.

The Gender Collective is responsible for drafting documents and publications, and organizing consulting sessions to support and guide women's specific work in the Movement.

Foster the participation of rural workers in unions and political parties

Convinced that agrarian reform and the conquest of the land do not depend only on the Movement's strength, the MST encourages coming together with the rest of trade-union rural workers to increase its power.

Aware that there will never be deep social changes without political instruments to guide and articulate the struggle, it stimulates the mass of rural workers to join left political parties.

Coordinate with city workers and Latin-American peasants

The Movement understands that all workers, in particular city workers – who are a much greater number – are interested in the struggle for the land and agrarian reform. Therefore, to create the correlation of forces necessary to produce the deep social changes required, it must coordinate with them in different ways, including support for the Single Workers' Trade Union (CUT). (18)

It also understands that many of the problems suffered by Brazilian workers are not the result of the economic situation of the country, but a consequence of world capitalist system and the specific policies of the United States for Latin America. So it believes it necessary to coordinate with all progressive forces of the continent, particularly the peasants, to face such a powerful enemy in better conditions.

III – ORGANIZATIONAL PRINCIPLES

In order to improve the organization's preparation to face the difficulties of the struggle itself, from the very beginning the MST attempted implementing a series of organizational principles and rules to avoid the errors already made by other social movements, many of which destroyed themselves because they committed many errors in their organizations. To quote only a few: personalized, charismatic and even religious leadership; very centralized structures; no training for cadres; deficient organization of conquered areas.

Colletive leadership

Starting with the national leadership, all MST instances have a collegiate leadership, and all members of collective leadership teams have "the same rights and power"; everything is decided by a majority vote. (19)

According to João Pedro Stedile, the chairman or secretary general of a peasant movement has only two possibilities: "either he is murdered or he betrays the movement. [...] Every chairman, even the least reformist one, can be easily coopted, through personal vanity or because he betrays his class. History [...] is full of examples of leaders who, having been previously launched by trade-union and popular organizations, have accepted a post as deputy or mayor. Some hold these posts to make class struggle go forward, but others are there only for their own personal benefit." (20) There resides the importance of not personalizing the main leadership of the Movement, but rather insisting on a collective one.

Division of tasks

The MST attempts to distribute tasks and functions among all the members at any organizational level whatsoever, so everyone can have a specific role and feel important. Everyone's participation is enhanced, thus avoiding the centralization of power, which often leads to individualistic deviations.

Tasks must be assigned according to the natural preferences of each person, so everyone can do what he feels most comfortable in.

The Movement has learned "that the first question you must ask a militant is: What would you like to do in the MST? A whole set of different skills and capacities can be found there. The organization then grows, because the members feel well in it; they are happy with what they are doing. Can you imagine the sacrifice it would be to ask teachers to organize a cooperative, or occupy a latifundium? No doubt, they wouldn't feel good about it, because of their personal characteristics. What they do like is to teach or do research, so that is the area in which they will make their contribution to the MST. That is possible only when there is a true division of tasks within the organization, because when it is centralized in only one person or group of people, this diversity is impossible, it does not open spaces for all those wishing to contribute to the struggle. There are people who are already retired, yet they look for us because they want to militate in the MST. That's fantastic! Not just because of the work these people will be doing within the Movement, but also because it shows they trust our organization, and above all, because they believe [in the ideals that inspire it]." (21)

Discipline

The MST believes internal discipline is nothing more than the respect for collective decisions. You can see it in both important and small matters, like always being on time. (22)

"If there isn't at least a little discipline, so people will respect decisions made at all echelons, you cannot build an organization. This is neither militarism nor authoritarianism; it's only one of the rules of democracy." There is no democracy without rules or regulations to control the behavior of the whole group. "Discipline consists in accepting the rules of the game. We have learned [this] from football and in the Catholic Church, which is one of the oldest organizations in the world. [...] If someone has joined the organization of his own free will, he must help define the rules and respect them; he must be disciplined, respect the collective. Otherwise, the organization will not grow." (23)

And one of those rules of the game is democratic centralism, which means a broad democratic discussion at all possible levels, but after voting, the minority must submit to the majority.

The Movement, however, avoids tight majorities to impose its will on those in the minority. If the large masses are not convinced, it is useless to impose something adopted by a small majority; it is better to wait for people to develop and become convinced that the measure in question is correct. Traditionally, the Movement implements only what has become a generalized feeling at the base. This avoids those terrible internal divisions that affect left movements and parties, and prevents important mistakes.

So, "when decisions are made within the Movement, they are generally unanimous. This is not written in the internal regulations, but [little by little] it has been understood that it is useless to insist when the vote is almost equally divided. The decision must ripen. If an idea wins by a small margin, either it becomes evident that the timing wasn't right, or it comes back with renewed strength. [...] Traditionally, the Movement implements only generalized feelings, thus avoiding huge mistakes." (24)

Wherever this is not put into practice, there are internal problems and the fight for agrarian reform is weakened.

Study
The Movement encourages its members to study everything related to its activities. "The person who does not know, is just like the person who does not see. And if you don't know, you can't lead." (25)

The organization will not go very far if it doesn't study. Study helps fight against voluntarism. It is not enough to kick the ball. "A football player can be very very good, but every day, after his tactical training, he must also train kicking penalty shots, otherwise he will not make a goal. The same thing happens with social struggle: you have to study [...]." (26)

Training cadres

Nowadays, when few social movements and political parties consider training cadres important, the MST highly values this activity, and believes it is one of its main pillars, because "the social organization that does not train its cadres has no future before it." Nobody outside the organization is going to train the necessary cadres, with the specific knowledge required: technical, political, cadres for organization, and professionals from all kinds of activity. (27)

Puts it: "Cadres must have scientific knowledge, be able to interpret the reality in which they both live and act – and from that specific knowledge, be able to transform reality. So this knowledge they acquire must include as many aspects as possible of human life", says Mário Lill, national MST leader. (28) "Cadres must understand both economy and personal relations or social policies. They must have a broad education, know about culture, religion. They must know how to interpret people's state of mind, work with them, building the new society we all want [...]." (29)

One of schooling's main aims is "to develop and guarantee political and ideological unity within the organization." (30)

On the other hand, these formative processes must contribute to the militants' revolutionary ethical stand, "based on values such as love for the people's cause, camaraderie, discipline, honesty, responsibility, criticism and self-criticism, dedication, solidarity, humility and devotion to the cause and the organization." (31)

This takes place not only during seminars and courses but also in the leaders' daily practice, during assemblies and meetings, mobilizations and occupations.

But how does the Movement form its cadres? Where does the content of this formation come from?

Learning from Brazil's experience in the struggle for land

The MST believes it is part of a "historical process of popular struggles," and it must therefore be humble enough to recognize that it must learn from previous activists. "They achieved their greatness only because they learned from those who came before them, and they were coherent with the past inherited from other fighters." (32)

Stedile wonders: "How is it possible to ignore the inheritance we were handed down by the martyrs of 500 years of struggle? We have invented nothing new. [...] Those who came before us made some errors and did some good things. We must learn from them, so as not to make the same errors and to repeat the good things they have done." (33)

For that reason, the Movement stresses the need for the historical recovery of Brazil's peasant struggles, as this will give an exact notion of the limitations and the temporary character of their participation.

"We have invented neither fire nor the wheel. We want to use what has already been invented [...] to build a better world." (34)

A broad but not dogmatic theoretical formation

The MST attempts to give a broad and not dogmatic theoretical formation to its cadres. This is yet another difference with the traditional left's evolution, which "has always been very dogmatic with the sources it has chosen to drink from [...]." (35)

"The cadre must have a very broad vision, not a closed or sectarian one; so the Movement drinks from all possible sources, and learns from all ideological currents, making every positive idea its own." (36)

According to one of its leaders, Theology for Liberation made a big contribution to this open-mindedness. In fact, this Theology "is a sort of symbiosis of different currents of thought, mixing Christianity with Marxism and with Latin-Americanism." That is what inspired the MST to be open to all truths.

"[…] All those who drank from Theology for Liberation – CPT, Catholics, Lutherans – taught us to practice open-mindedness to all doctrines that speak up for the people. This vision of the world gave us the open-minded attitude we needed to find those who could help us," declares Stedile. (37)

On the other hand, the concrete practice of the struggle for agrarian reform taught the MST that "you can't copy other people's experiences, because each space, each local reality, come with new elements that grow out of accumulated knowledge." (38)

Formation received by the majority of the better cadres

We must not forget that several of the Movement's more prepared cadres received a progressive education, not in left political parties but in seminaries of the Catholic Church. Very often, the priesthood was the only way a peasant child could study beyond elementary school.

The Gospel

The Gospel was very much a presence in the beginning – and in many places it still is – "not as a religion, but as a doctrine with influence on values, culture, and the way mystique is viewed." (39)

Influence of Marxist classics

Though the MST is open to the most diverse currents of thought, "the philosophical and scientific guideline" for its struggle in favor of social transformation is "Marxism." (40)

They read Marx, Engels, Lenin, Rose Luxemburg, Mao Tse Tung, and the MST takes what is useful from these authors and discards what is not. It has never adhered dogmatically to any classic thinker.

Influence of Brazilian and Latin-American classics

But the better-formed cadres in the MST have studied not only Marxist classics but also those of their own country (41) and of Latin America (42), as well as world political leaders (43) and other contemporary authors. (44)

Using national events

The MST also uses its national events to "allow its militants to meet academicians, specialists and top-level professors. Usually they are university professors, renowned personalities or national politicians. Thanks to these meetings, the militants become aware of the important debates within the MST and the political world in the country." (45)

Learning from political and social leaders and their oral presentations

Another very interesting method used by the MST to form its cadres are the international events the left organizes in the country (São Paulo Forum; World Social Forum; PT and CUT congresses, and others), that convoke an important number of political leaders from different countries. The MST invites them to talk with its main cadres. An important aspect is that they invite personalities from different ideological and political positions – contrary to the traditional left's attitude of listening only to those who support its own convictions or study them in depth.

Method used in forming people

Formation takes off from what people themselves put into practice. Then comes a theoretical analysis related to that practice and – together with the conclusions reached by the people involved in the process – they rerout and correct that same practice, which is now transformed. There is a perpetual pendulum between practice-theory-practice. (46)

Relationship with the base

There is yet another principle followed by the MST: a strong relationship between the leaders and the base. "No matter how important the leader is, no matter what he has studied, no matter how combative and active he is, if he doesn't keep his feet on the ground, if he doesn't develop […] his ties with the social base, he won't go very far." (47)

Some time ago the MST required a specific percentage of its leaders – even those from the National Leadership – to live on a settlement, but later on it understood this doesn't necessarily mean the leader is related to the social base.

Vilson Santin is one of the MST's national leaders who lives on a settlement; he believes it is a very enriching experience but it also represents huge challenges. In his opinion, "you must make a big effort and not fall into a rut, and avoid being influenced by the environment." The positive part is that the leader "feels the problems personally, he must face these things, so his proposals are really down to earth."

The MST must also create its own mechanisms to listen and consult, "drink" from the people's strength and determination – that is the best way to avoid errors. "A leader estranged from the masses is like a fish without water." (48)

Planning

Another MST characteristic resides in the fact that it is not only one of the most disciplined movements in Latin America – it is also one of those that work most efficiently. This is possible only by planning activities ahead and in detail, always weighing the results to correct errors and deviations, and be able to overcome them in future activities.

Criticism and self-criticism

Criticism and self-criticism are very related to the previous principle, for it is very important for the Movement and its different instances, and its members individually, to humbly evaluate their work, trying to correct errors for future events.

Professionalism

Finally, it is important for all those who accept carrying out one of the Movement's tasks, to do so as professionally and seriously as possible, with love and total devotion, becoming real "specialists" of that activity.

IV – ORGANIZATIONAL STRUCTURE

The MST has been very careful to avoid a rigid and inflexible organizational structure, so it has adapted, modified and transformed it according to the Movement's needs, timing and development.

We will now describe present-day structure and, whenever necessary, there will be a note explaining the transformations in a specific instance.

GROUPS OF FAMILIES: THE BASIC ORGANIZATIONAL CELL

Family groups

As we have already observed in the chapter on camps, the MST basic structure are the groups of families, which function in all camps. Since we are in a permanent struggle and future steps are discussed day after day, all the families are organized by groups of affinities, and all together they analyze decisions to be made. The Movement wants these family groups to continue their work in the settlements, but for reasons already discussed, so far this has been possible only in a small number of them.

These family groups are the social base of the Movement.

Work and militant commissions

As we have seen in their respective chapters, in both camps

and settlements there are commissions for the different activities: health, negotiation, school, security, work etc. They are made up by one or more representatives from each family group interested in developing that specific activity. Usually, they are people more eager than others to dedicate themselves to the Movement. For example, if health activities require an hour a day, these people take the task on but devote their time in an unlimited way. They are also available for any task the MST requires in other parts of the country. (49) These people are considered militants of the Movement.

At present, some leaders believe the best thing would be for each member of a family group to accept a specific responsibility, because they would have to assume this seriously, give an account of their activity before their group, and all this would increase their self-esteem and contribute to their awareness and political development. (50)

A representative from each commission of the camp or settlement becomes a member of the regional, state or national commission of that sector. Its members range between 5 and 15 and they function as a permanent commission for that specific activity. (51)

Atempt to create nuclei of militants

In 1990, when the organization of family groups wasn't yet consolidated, the Movement attempted to create nuclei of militants – a structure that would make it possible to group the people closest to the MST – but the experience wasn't positive. The idea wasn't bad, but apparently the timing was not right. And since the MST social base wasn't well consolidated, those militants became isolated and lost contact with the base. According to Vilson Santin, "at that time, the important thing was to have a proposal to organize all the families, and that the militants work with the Movement's grassroots, always close to them." (52)

In fact, the militants already participated in the activities organized by the commissions existing in each MST sector: they prepared new occupations or organized the camp, if they belonged to the Commission for the Masses; prepared courses, analyzing teaching methods, if they belonged to the Commission for Education; drafted press bulletins and other communiqués, if they were in the Commission for Communications and Propaganda; and so forth for all the other commissions (53), and it became very hard for them to find time for family group meetings and those of nuclei of militants.

New method to cohere militants

At present, because of the critical situation the MST finds itself in as a result of the measures adopted by the Cardoso Administration and which we have already mentioned – including the negative campaign in the mass media – the Movement is studying once again the possibility of organizing its militants so they can react better to this situation.

Today, the number one task of the MST is to increase the ideological education of its social base, so they will be able to resist the economic and ideological war waged against it. The landless peasants must be prepared for a long struggle, whose results won't always be immediately evident. So it must qualify its militants, who must learn to work with the family groups not concentrating their attention only on the practical problems that come up in the camps or settlements – as was the case in the past – but also on giving that group of peasants the information they need to understand what is going on in the country, with sufficient arguments to avoid their being confused by this campaign in the mass media.

They are implementing a new method to work with the militants. It includes the creation of a National Commission for Formation, made up of 50 people with two representatives from each state; they meet every two months to prepare documents, discuss different topics etc. Each state also has around 20 to 30 coordinators to monitor the formation of the nuclei of militants, so each monitor can coordinate a nucleus made up of 20 to 50 militants, depending on the size of the settlement, the distances etc. These nuclei should meet every 15 days for a political debate; to analyze and discuss the newspapers, local problems and actions for the future. The MST already has 470 monitors all over the country and it hopes to organize around 20 000 militants before the year 2001 comes to an end. (54)

The coordinators of these nuclei also organize courses, seminars, and related events. (55)

Courses or Schools for the Formation of Militants have been created for those new members of the MST who wish to work for the Movement but either don't really know how to, or don't have the necessary qualification. (56)

REPRESENTATIVE AND DELIBERATIVE INSTANCES

National level

National Congress
The National Congress is the main MST instance. Every five years it convenes militants from all the states where the Movement is organized. They have been previously elected in state meetings, according to a specific number determined at the national level, which takes into account the amount of families settled or camped. The total number of delegates to the meeting or to the Congress is established each time, trying to convene as many delegates as possible. In general, more than 5000 delegates participate in MST congresses. In the last one, there were 11 725 delegates.

These congresses must adopt the general guidelines – already discussed in different instances – and aim at fraternal relations and unity of MST members for common objectives. (57)

National Meetings

The MST holds national meetings every two years.

Representatives from each state (who are members of the National Coordination) participate in these meetings together with the National Settlers' Commission; national teams, sectors and commissions, and a representative from each state's Secretariats. The number of these delegates varies each time: it has fluctuated between 200 and 1500. But since it is very difficult to move so many people in such a huge country, recently it was decided to have regional meetings, and once a year, a national meeting with only three representatives from each state. (58)

These meetings define the platforms for the immediate struggle, according to the specific timing for the Movement's needs. These proposals and suggestions have been previously analyzed in state meetings.

The definitions emanating from this national meeting related to national policies, must be respected by all MST instances.

National Coordination

It is the Movement's highest instance of direction.

It is responsible for the implementation of the resolutions adopted in national congresses and meetings. All political decisions of a national nature affecting the Movement are made by this instance, which must also guarantee the application of its principles, publicly answer for it, and be responsible for its finances. Finally, the National Coordination must promote the Movement's articulation in new states. (60)

The National Coordination, however, doesn't decide everything the states must do. On the contrary, each municipality and each state are autonomous in their decision-making. "All municipal, regional or state commissions – wherever they are – have complete autonomy and power of decision. It is the comrades at the base who decide everything they must do." (61) These local bodies are guided by a general policy, but the way they implement it "is completely decentralized." (62) "What is expected – and stimulated – in the implementation of the program and political guidelines is creativity and decentralization. One of the general guidelines, for example, is that everyone should carry out occupations, but not necessarily with the same method – rather, each individual place must find the most adequate way to organize the occupation and the right timing for it." (63)

The main lines are discussed at the national or state level, where they also analyze if they are following the correct path. And the behavior of the enemy forces: the large landowners and the government, is also the center of specific analysis.

They also look into the smaller general things the Movement can do in all states: study notebooks, assemblies, meetings or manifestations.

This instance is made up by two members from each state, elected by the State Executive or the Movement's State Meeting; by the members of the National Leadership and the instance in charge of the settlers (64), which probably by the year 2002 will be known as the Sector for Production, Cooperation and the Environment.

A member of this future sector also participates from each state as well as two members from each sector of activity.

The National Coordination must meet every three months, and exceptionally whenever necessary. (65)

The decisions are the result of public vote and they are adopted by a simple majority. (66)

National Leadership

The National Leadership is where the Movement's political positions are drafted and discussed, guaranteeing that its aims will be pursued as foreseen. It must safeguard its coherence and political unity as well as its growing autonomy, avoiding "dependence on other bodies for its existence, most particularly its finances." (67) At the same time, it must plan the strategies and tactics to be submitted to the National Coordination, study the political and practical needs of the Movement and propose solutions. (68)

To be responsible for the Movement's main instance "doesn't mean to rule over it, but rather to have a general vision of what is happening in the country and inform the bases about these discussions, so the MST will always be in harmony with its main objectives, organizing the necessary struggles to attain them." (69)

The National Leadership is made up of a number of members that varies – around 21 people, who are elected by direct and secret votes during national meetings. Each delegate can vote for 21 names, submitted individually and not on ballots. Those who get more than 51% of the votes are then elected; if someone doesn't get this percentage he isn't elected, so there are times when the Leadership has less than 21 members.

The candidates are sponsored by at least 25 signatures or by the previous national leadership. In each state, generally the different instances submit the names of those comrades they believe to be better qualified and experienced for this.

Though the candidates are not submitted because of gender or geographic criteria, once elected they are distributed by state and sector of activity. (70)

There is no rule defining quotas for women. Their weight or presence in the leadership depends exclusively on their work during the struggle. The present National Leadership has 22 members, nine of whom are women (40%), thanks to the permanent interest in promoting women's participation in all MST instances, sectors and activities. (72).

The militants who make up the national leadership must have the following characteristics:

– have an in-depth knowledge of what a mass movement is all about;

– know the national situation and how to analyze their society;

– be ideologically firm;

– be disciplined;

– be able to increase their theoretical knowledge in history, economy, politics and other topics;

– be able to develop collective practice;

– know how to plan and coordinate activities;

– be able to make decisions;

– be able to articulate both the struggles and the organization.

Though the tasks of the National Leadership can't be carried out by just any militant, the MST has decided to start qualifying working militants of the Movement so they will increase their incorporation in the different leadership instances. (73)

The National Leadership meets every two months and it must prepare the meetings for the National Coordination. (74)

Characteristics of the terms

Two-year renewable terms

Internal norms define two-year terms for those who are elected. This could be a problem because they must hold elections every two years, but the method has turned out to be quite pedagogic. (75) Once the term is over, the leaders go through a deep evaluation, and if the results are positive, they stay on. With this method there is no feeling of being eternal.

A leader can be reelected "depending on the internal evaluation the MST will make of the candidate's activity during his mandate, the needs of the organization, and his availability. (76)

Though there is no fixed or preestablished rule as far as the renewal of the leaders' mandate, it has become a common practice in each election to renew around 30% of the members, thus allowing the incorporation of new leaders and new references for society.

Anyone can resign during his mandate or be discharged as a

result of a decision made by the corresponding instances. A mandate is not a sacred thing, nor is the elected person untouchable.

Local instances

State meetings

State meetings take place once a year to evaluate political guidelines, activities and actions carried out by the MST. Activities are also planned there and they elect the members of the state and national coordinations.

State coordinations

State coordinations are composed by members who are elected during state meetings. They are responsible for implementing MST political guidelines, for the sectors of activities and for the actions the State meetings plan.

State leaderships

State leaderships have a varying number of members, designated by the coordinations at the same level. They are in charge of those who represent MST regions in each state, and the organic aspects and development of the sectors of activities.

EXECUTIVE INSTANCES

Both national and state secretariats are the Movement's operational instances, whose members are nonelected cadres qualified for these responsibilities.

INSTANCES BY ACTIVITIES

Sectors and other collective groups

As we have already explained, with the establishment of the

first camps, work commissions were created to guarantee survival and continue the struggle for the land. They included health, education, security, work, communications and supplies commissions. This is how different sectors of activities came up with their respective commissions.

On the other hand, when the campers were able to get land and became settlers, they had to maintain their organization to solve problems that affected the whole settler community. Some of these problems were the same as those in camps, like children's education and health; others were the result of the challenge due to the new situation: the need for efficient production, sell their goods, get credit etc. So new sectors of activities come up with their respective commissions, like the ones for production and finances.

As the MST continued growing and with it the number of camps and settlements throughout the country, it became necessary to improve planning the work of each sector of activity, and this is why local, regional, state and national sectors were born.

At present there are sectors for Training; Media and Propaganda; Finances; Education; Health; Mass Movement, also known as Mass Front; Production; Projects; and Human Rights. At the national level there is also a Sector for International Relations, and they are about to create the Sector for Production, Cooperation and the Environment, to substitute the Concrab Sector for Settlements, "as a way to increase its activities and include aspects that were not taken up by any specific sector, like the environment and transgenic seeds." (77)

Organization is flexible, each state can create other sectors when it deems it necessary.

Mass Front: the heart of the MST

From the very first struggles that gave way to the MST, there has been work with the masses, but it wasn't until 1984 when it became institutionalized in the Mass Front sector, after the MST became a movement with national scope. That year, work began to prepare cadres for this activity.

The Mass Front is not just one more sector or activity of the MST, as we have already said, it is its very heart, "pumping blood to the whole movement." It unites cadres working at the base, and all those who expand the Movement to the whole country. (78)

Because so many activists are needed for that front, what usually happens when they discover a camp with a potentially militant group of campers and a very low cultural level, to gain time they promote training courses for that group in the camp itself.

Concrab and the Sector for Settlements

The National Commission for Settlements became Concrab and, in a process where only the name changed, they created the Sector for Settlements. Today, they are thinking of changing its name to Sector for Production, Cooperation and the Environment.

There are also groups of women – we have already talked about them – and culture, which have worked to recover the original values of the artistic and cultural production of landless peasants. They make compact disks and act throughout the states to promote popular culture.

V – How the MST finances itself

We have already spoken about how the MST, concerned about its autonomy as a social movement, practiced self-financing as much as possible.

We will now describe the sources of these resources.

Resources from obligatory contributions

National and state leaderships are financed by collections the MST organizes in the settlements, based on the principle that those families who have already received land and credits must cooperate with the Movement so agrarian reform can reach all corners of the country.

Each settled family must contribute 1% of its yearly production for the Movement.

According to MST norms, all settlements are encouraged to contribute up to 4% of their production, but in each state – and therefore in each settlement – they themselves decide the percentage of the contribution, according to existing conditions and their economic situation. Other settlements and cooperatives sometimes make their contribution with food, vehicles, or liberating militants for other tasks in the Movement.

OTHER FORMS OF COLLECTION

Besides these taxes, there are other ways to collect resources.

The activities foreseen for this can be insignificant, but if they are continuous and concrete they do have results; for example, small businesses not requiring a complex organization, like the sale of agricultural products and arts and crafts; recovery and development of available natural resources.

Massive campaigns are also organized among the Movement's social base (donating products or work days) and the urban middle class (bonds, products, shows, sale of educational and cultural materials). Sebastião Salgado's international photo campaign had a great repercussion, since the photographer donated his work to support the MST. Practically every year, several artists donate their work to the Movement as a way to practice their solidarity.

This policy includes looking for local official resources, knocking on governmental offices's doors (Agricultural Departments, universities, banks). The MST attempts to rerout part of these resources to other sectors of activities, such as education, training, technical assistance, health – all of which should be state concerns, but if they are also developed by the MST, they increase their importance.

All militants are involved in this campaign to collect money at specific times of the year.

There is a permanent show of solidarity from many groups of MST friends, as well as from cooperation bodies abroad, not necessarily of a religious nature. This foreign support has contributed to the development of essential activities and it has been very important for the Movement and the practice of internationalist solidarity.

Whenever possible, the MST practices effective solidarity with landless groups in other countries, like peasant groups from Latin-American countries and African Portuguese-speaking countries.

PLANNING FINANCES

The Movement drafts and implements economic and financial plans and others for the collection of resources in each one of its instances. From family groups up to the commissions in the settlements, and state commissions and sectors, everyone of them should be self-financed.

Where resources go to

The MST's financial policy is transparent.

Seventy percent of all resources collected in the state through different taxes goes to state activities, while the other 30% is for national ones.

The national leadership is responsible for defining where these resources go to, while state executives do so taking into account the priorities defined in state and national meetings.

The resources are fundamentally channelled to guarantee the Movement's organization, infrastructure and activities: conditions in secretariats and training centers, means of communication and transportation and other aspects that will allow the MST to act as the efficient and strong organization it is meant to be.

To supervise the use of finances in each state, the MST has created controlling councils, which must also correct the incorrect way money is being used. Every three months, the financial teams must give a detailed report of the money collected and the way it has been invested.

One of the principles of this Movement is that all activities for mass struggle, mobilizations etc., must be financed by the base itself, since there resides the guarantee for its autonomy and the responsibility shared between them. If a movement requires resources from outside to organize a mobilization or some kind of struggle, it will be tied to this dependence and its struggling capacities alienated. So the MST tries to make the people understand that the struggle depends on their own resources. Only then will these struggles educate and contribute to the political development of these comrades.

Liberation of militants

As we have seen, the MST wants settlements to liberate militants for other organizational and political activities of the Movement. Most settlements liberate one or more cadres who will work full time for the Movement and their agricultural work is taken over by the rest of the members.

Every two years there is an evaluation of their work, and it is decided whether the cadres will continue their task or go back to production.

NOTES

1. João Pedro Stedile, Bernardo Mançano Fernandes, *Brava Gente...*, Ediciones Barbarroja, Buenos Aires, April 2000, p. 36; Brazilian edition *Brava Gente...*, Editora Perseu Abramo, São Paulo, 1999, p. 31.
2. In Brazil they are called *posseiros.*

3. "The law [...] said that when the size (in modules) of a piece of property was smaller than what would be necessary for the food and progress of a family, it would be considered a 'minifundium'," J. P. Stedile, *Latifúndio: o pecado agrário brasileiro*, 1999, unprinted document.

4. Ivonete Tonin, Coordinator for the state of Rio Grande do Sul, interview by Marta Harnecker, November 16, 2001.

5. J. P. Stedile, *Latifúndio: o pecado agrário brasileiro*, 1999, unprinted document.

6. Roseli Salete Caldart, *Pedagogia do...*, op. cit., p. 87.

7. MST, *Reforma Agrária: por um Brasil sem latifúndio!*, 2000, p. 26.

8. J. P. Stedile, B. Mançano Fernandes, *Brava Gente...*, op. cit., p. 40; Braz. Edit., p. 35.

9. Op. cit., p. 42; Braz. Edit., p. 36.

10. Op. cit., p. 40; Braz. Edit., p. 34.

11. Frei Flávio, interview by Marta Harnecker, Porto Alegre, May 2001.

12. Ibidem.

13. *Reforma agrária: por um Brasil sem latifúndio*, op. cit., p. 25.

14. This topic will be developed further on.

15. This is how they describe it in their booklet: "Devote yourself to train leaders and prepare a political leadership made up of workers."

16. *Normas gerais do MST*, September 1989. On this topic see pp. 22-23.

17. Ivonete Tonin, interview by..., op. cit.

18. According to the decision of the Second National Meeting of the Movement, January 1986, the Movement supported the CUT. See: *Normas gerais...*, September 1989, p. 10.

19. *Normas gerais...*, op.cit., p. 19.

20. J. P. Stedile, B. Mançano Fernandes, *Brava Gente...*, op. cit., p. 47; Braz. Edit., pp. 39-40.

21. Op. cit., p. 49; Braz. Edit., p. 41.

22. *Normas gerais...*, op. cit., p. 20.

23. J. P. Stedile, B. Mançano Fernandes, *Brava Gente...*, op. cit., pp. 50-51; Braz. Edit., pp. 41-42.

24. Op.cit., p. 99, Braz. Edit., p. 85.

25. *Normas gerais...*, op. cit., p. 20.

26. J. P. Stedile, B. Mançano Fernandes, *Brava Gente...*, op. cit., p. 50; Braz. Edi., p. 41.

27. Op. cit., pp. 50-51; Braz. Edit., pp. 42-43.
28. Mário Luis Lill, ex chairman of Iterra, interview by Marta Harnecker, Brazil, 2000.
29. Ibidem.
30. Ibidem.
31. *MST, Documento básico do MST*, op. cit., p. 45.
32. J. P. Stedile, B. Mançano Fernandes, *Brava Gente*..., op. cit., p. 69; Braz. Edit., p. 58.
33. Op. cit., p. 68; Braz. Edit., p. 57.
34. Op. cit., p. 69; Braz. Edit., p. 58.
35. Ibidem.
36. Mário Luis Lill, interview..., op. cit.
37. J. P. Stedile, B. Mançano Fernandes, *Brava Gente*..., op. cit., p. 70; Braz. Edit., p. 59.
38. Op. cit., pp. 69-70, Braz. Edit., pp. 58-59.
39. Op. cit., p. 72; Braz. Edit., p. 60.
40. Mário Luis Lill, interview..., op. cit.
41. Outstanding among Brazilian philosophers are Josué de Castro, Manuel Correia, Celso Furtado, Florestan Fernandes, Darci Ribeiro, Paulo Freire, Luiz Carlos Prestes, Correa Andrade and Leonardo Boff, and others. (J. P. Stedile, B. Mançano Fernandes, *Brava Gente*..., op. cit., pp. 72-73, Braz. Edit., pp. 60-62).
42. Che Guevara, José Martí, Julio César Sandino, Fidel Castro, Emiliano Zapata.
43. Nelson Mandela, Mahatma Ghandi, Martin Luther King, Patrice Lumumba, Agostinho Neto, Samora Machel, Amilcar Cabral.
44. James Petras, Marta Harnecker (J. P. Stedile, B. Mançano Fernandes, *Brava Gente*..., op. cit., p. 72; Braz. Edit., p. 60.
45. Op. cit., p. 97; Braz. Edit., p. 83.
46. MST, *Documento básico do MST*, Piracicaba, February 1991, p. 44. This idea of *practice-theory-practice* is nothing other than the dialectic methodology on which Popular Education is based. It means starting off from the concrete reality of the people and how they live through it; analyze its causes and consequences from a global point of view, and then go back to practice, only this time in a different way, with consequent actions to transform it.
47. J. P. Stedile, B. Mançano Fernandes, *Brava Gente*..., op. cit., p. 51; Braz. Edit., p. 43.

48. *Normas gerais...*, op. cit., p. 20.
49. Christiane Campos, interview by Marta Harnecker, Montreal, February 2001.
50. Ivonete Tonin, interview..., op. cit.
51. J. P. Stedile, Letter to Marta Harnecker, April 5, 2001.
52. Vilson Santin, interview by Marta Harnecker, Montreal, April 2001.
53. J. P. Stedile, Letter to..., op. cit.
54. J. P. Stedile, Letter to..., op. cit.
55. Ibidem.
56. Christiane Campos, interview..., op. cit.
57. *Normas gerais...*, op. cit., pp. 13-14.
58. Ivonete Tonin, interview..., op. cit.
59. *Normas gerais...*, op.cit., p. 14.
60. Op. cit., p. 15.
61. MST, *Construindo...*, op. cit., p. 57.
62. J. P. Stedile, B. Mançano Fernandes, *Brava Gente...*, op. cit., p. 103; Braz. Edit., p. 89.
63. Op. cit., p. 103; Braz. Edit., p. 90.
64. *Normas gerais...*, op. cit., p. 15.
65. Ibidem.
66. Ibidem.
67. MST, *Construindo...*, op. cit., p. 60.
68. *Normas gerais...*, op. cit., pp. 15-16.
69. MST, *Construindo...*, op.cit., pp. 59-60.
70. J. P. Stedile, Notes to this chapter, December 28, 2001.
71. *Normas gerais...*, op. cit., p. 16.
72. J. P. Stedile, B. Mançano Fernandes, *Brava Gente...*, op. cit., p. 106; Braz. Edit., pp. 91-92.
73. MST, *Construindo...*, op. cit., p. 59.
74. *Normas gerais...*, op.cit., p. 16. See also MST, *Construindo...*, op. cit., p. 58.
75. J. P. Stedile, P. Mançano Fernandes, *Brava Gente...*, op. cit., p. 105; Braz. Edit., pp. 90-91.
76. Op. cit., p. 106; Braz. Edit., p. 91.
77. J. P. Stedile, Notes to this chapter, op. cit.
78. Christiane Campos, interview..., op.cit.

Impressão e acabamento

Cromosete
GRÁFICA E EDITORA LTDA.
Rua Uhland, 307 - Vila Ema
Cep: 03283-000 · São Paulo · SP
Tel/Fax: 011 6104-1176

1   2   3   4   5   6   7   8   9   10